FROM ROYALTY TO REVOLUTION

THE SUN URANUS RELATIONSHIP

Other books by Glenn Perry

Introduction to AstroPsychology
A Synthesis of Modern Astrology & Depth Psychology

Mapping the Landscape of the Soul
Inside Psychological Astrology

Depth Analysis of the Natal Chart
Advanced Therapeutic Astrology

The Shadow in the Horoscope
Five Essays on Jung's Concept of the Shadow

Stealing Fire from the Gods
New Directions in Astrological Research

Issues & Ethics
In the Profession of Astrology

From Ancient to Postmodern Astrology
An Evolution of Ideas, Techniques & Perspectives

FROM ROYALTY TO REVOLUTION

THE SUN URANUS RELATIONSHIP

GLENN PERRY

AAP Press

East Hampton, CT • www.aaperry.com

Copyright © 2012 by AAP Press

All rights reserved. Printed in the United States of America. No part of this book may be reproduced in any manner whatsoever without written permission except in the case of brief quotations embodied in critical articles and reviews. For information, address AAP Press, 133 Injun Hollow, Haddam Neck, CT 06424.

ISBN: 061563401X
ISBN-13: 978-0615634012

*In memory of my friend
and mentor, Richard Idemon*

CONTENTS

	Preface	xi
1	**From Royalty to Revolution** *The Marriage of Leo and Aquarius*	1
2	**The Hero and the Trickster** *Archetypal Functions of the Sun and Uranus*	37
3	**Noble King, Wise Fool** *Aspects between the Sun and Uranus*	75
	References	128

Acknowledgments

I would like to express my gratitude to Twink McKenney for her visionary skills in helping design the cover of *From Royalty to Revolution*. Also, I have been fortunate to have Gina Bostian's expertise in formatting the book and for her support and encouragement along the way. Thanks are also due to the entire Design Team at Createspace for their earnest determination in getting the book to press expeditiously. Finally, I want to thank my many friends and colleagues in the astrological community for their encouragement in bringing this manuscript to print.

Preface

This book explores the archetypal meaning of the Leo-Aquarius polarity, and delineates the deeper significance of aspects between their respective rulers—the Sun and Uranus. Just as the Sun resides at the heart of the solar system, so also it symbolizes the heart and will of the individual. The purpose of the Sun is to develop self-esteem and a bounded, well-defined sense of self. The antithesis of the Sun, however, is the planet Uranus, which signifies the need for detachment and liberation from fixed definitions of self. Integrating these opposite but ultimately complementary processes is the key to both personal and collective evolution.

As the ruler of Leo, the Sun represents a set of interrelated psychological functions represented in myth and literature by specific archetypes—the Ruler, the Creator, and the Hero. Likewise, as the ruler of Aquarius, Uranus signifies certain functions that are embodied in the archetype of the Trickster, or Fool, which is the natural counterpart to solar images. Whereas the solar principle leads to self-esteem and the construction of a personal identity, Uranus invites identification with the cosmic will and thereby awakens the self to a transpersonal, collective identity.

If unintegrated, aspects between these two planets can indicate an unstable self-image, schizoid disorder, and perverse rebelliousness—or, resistance to change and compensatory egotism. If well integrated, however, these same aspects symbolize a capacity for conscious evolution, recognition of impermanence, and emancipation from the dictates of pride. Full integration enables one to be led by a higher intelligence for the sake of the collective good.

Chapter One

From Royalty to Revolution

THE MARRIAGE OF LEO AND AQUARIUS

The self-concept and its affective component, self-esteem, have probably received more press in contemporary psychological literature than any other idea. It enters with increasing frequency into popular parlance, appears in the press, on soap operas, and even in governmental debate. How the self-concept is determined and developed is a source of endless discussion. Numerous social science studies have documented a link between low self-esteem and social ills such as drug and alcohol abuse, juvenile delinquency, violent crime, poverty, spousal abuse, and job failure. This led to the creation in 1986 of the California State Task Force to Promote Self-Esteem. Clearly, the development of a positive self-concept is important to health and happiness.

Psychologists define the self-concept as the totality of the individual's thoughts and feelings with reference to himself as an object. Yet, a central tenet of Buddhist philosophy and myriad other sacred traditions is that we have no permanent identity. What Buddhists call the self, or *sattva*, is said to be merely an illusion of separateness. Identity is a construction of the human mind and is subject to continuous change into more complex states until, finally, it awakens to the realization that it is an extension of a Cosmic Mind. In Chapter One, we will explore this process of evolutionary change primarily through an analysis of Leo and Aquarius. I will argue that Leo is the motive force for building an identity, while Aquarius symbolizes the need for awakening the self to its connection with Universal Mind.

Leo & Aquarius as Motivational Needs

A good place to begin our analysis is by defining what we mean by Leo and Aquarius. Zodiacal signs are best understood from an archetypal perspective, meaning they are universal thought forms of an objective psyche, or cosmic mind, that precipitate down as organizing principles of nature itself. As such, they are non-local entities that structure not only human consciousness but also related processes on social, biological, and material levels. An astrological sign, therefore, can have a variety of meanings. Psychologically, it symbolizes a basic human need, developmental stage, behavioral style, and affiliated emotions. Because archetypes can manifest in diverse ways across the entire spectrum of human experience—from inner motivation to outer event—they are protean entities that serve as unifying psychological principles.

It is important to differentiate signs from their popularization as personality types. As soon as you place a planet in a sign, you change the expression of that sign. The nature of a planet will always tend to shape the sign in the direction of that planet's agenda. The Sun, for example, will make a sign more prideful and expressive. If the Sun is in Aquarius, then Aquarius will tend to manifest more colorfully than it would, for example, if the Moon resided in this sign. Sun in Aquarius is more likely to display zany, provocative, or outrageous behavior, yet these traits have as much to do with the Sun as with Aquarius. With Sun in Aquarius the individual's pride is linked to how creative s/he can be *within the Aquarian domain*—implementing change, promoting reform, or championing a cause. Yet, if one analyzes the core themes of Aquarius that reappear across planetary positions, its meaning can be differentiated from the nature of the planets that animate it.

The same, of course, goes for Leo. Thus in the descriptions that follow, the reader should note that I am not describing Leo or Aquarius as personality types.* Rather, I am describing Leo and Aquarius as pure, archetypal entities that manifest as psychological needs, traits, states, attitudes, and perspectives independent of any planet that may tenant them.

LEO AS THE NEED FOR SELF-ESTEEM

Perhaps the most fundamental meaning of signs is their significance as human motives. The motive of a sign can be inferred from behavior that is characteristic of that sign. There are several interrelated themes for Leo, just as there are for Aquarius. Leo's most salient quality is extroversion. There is an innate expressiveness to Leo, almost a peacock quality, as if it enjoys nothing more than being itself. Leo is regal, proud, and confident. It loves to perform. This quality of self-love is paralleled by an equally strong appreciation of others. Whenever Leo focuses its attention on you, there is a feeling of being bathed in radiant warmth. The expression "everyone loves a lover" is applicable to Leo, for it is enormously charming, social, and playful. Leo behavior is designed to win people over; it is, in effect, "winning behavior." No sign is more gregarious and affable. This is perhaps best exemplified in courtship and romance where the goal is to get the beloved to associate

---

* Personally I abhor typologies, including and especially Sun sign astrology. If astrology teaches us one thing, it's that people should not be typed. Every chart is a unique blend of zodiacal factors. It follows that every individual is a unique being.

her good feelings with being in the company of the suitor. Naturally chivalrous and gracious, Leo makes you feel good about *you*.

The natural flash and showmanship of the sign makes it singularly adept at gaining attention. Leo's desire for the limelight and its presumption of importance naturally incline it to positions of leadership—to be *the boss*. If the presumption of importance is carried too far, however, Leo behavior is subject to conceit and self-aggrandizement. This part of us is preoccupied with externals, i.e., with popularity, image, and the like. Leo loves to put on a good show and impress others with its style if not its substance. This, in turn, is related to Leo's susceptibility to flattery and its primary psychological blind-spot: the inability to accurately assess another's character. A notoriously poor judge of people, Leo's need to be liked presupposes it to see the best in others, and this makes it easy prey to hucksters, fawners, and deceivers.

By being amiable, Leo increases the probability that its friendliness will be reciprocated—i.e., that the other will "like" him/her. Again, this is a primary goal behind Leo behavior. It is precisely because this part of human nature is so vulnerable to loss of esteem that it rages against injuries to its pride. Leo's stubborn defensiveness and lack of forgiveness operates as a defense against any implication that it is not superior. Accordingly, Leo is subject to the divinity complex—difficulty admitting fallibility, tolerating defeat, admitting wrongdoing, or backing down from an argument. Leo takes itself very seriously and abhors humiliation or criticism of any kind. This arrogant defensiveness makes it prone to a double standard, or what has been referred to as the divine right of kings: Leo gives itself absolute clemency in wrongdoing, yet is absolutely unforgiving to enemies.

From these and other related qualities we can infer two primary motives that underlie Leo behavior: (1) the need for validation, approval, and attention, all of which contribute to self-esteem—the primary motive; and (2) the need for play, creativity, and **self-expression**, which is the secondary motive. Obviously, without some form of creative self-expression one cannot attract the attention, validation, and approval that are necessary for building self-esteem.

Aquarius as The Need for Awakening

Just as Leo can be deconstructed to reveal the core psychological needs that underlay its various permutations, so the basic needs that Aquarius symbolizes can be inferred from its characteristic forms and behaviors. Perhaps the most salient quality of Aquarius is its capacity for objectivity. Aquarius evidences an aloof detachment that allows it to see truly because, unlike Leo, it has no investment in what it sees.

Whereas Leo is warm and validating, Aquarius can be cool and distant. If Leo signifies romantic love, Aquarius represents brotherly and sisterly love, or what the Greeks called *agape*. This is an impersonal friendliness that one individual feels for another simply because the other is human. Aquarius does not judge, "like me, good, not like me, bad," as Leo does. Rather, Aquarius perceives and, indeed, expects every individual to be totally unique.

Accordingly, Aquarius is open-minded, tolerant, and egalitarian. Instead of getting caught in the trap of conformity to a social or cultural standard, Aquarius transcends the differences that artificially separate one group from another. This part of our nature is identified with humanity itself.

Aquarius displays a tremendous capacity for originality because it is not concerned with validation or approval and therefore is radically open to alternative ways of being. Its uniqueness of perspective is, in part, a consequence of a marked lack of concern for any externally imposed condition of acceptance. Thus liberated from the straightjacket of normalcy, Aquarius is *free* to be anyone or anything. Behavior does not need to be consistent, and identity is not limited to a particular style or outlook. This gives Aquarius its penchant for eccentric and erratic behavior.

The ability to see novel possibilities and generate new ideas confers a certain brilliance to this sign. Aquarius represents our capacity for wholistic thinking. Like a wide-angle lens, it instantly sees how all the parts make up the whole. In fact, it is precisely the whole that occupies the Aquarian view—the whole of anything, e.g., a body, psyche, family, government, society, species, or universe. This "God's-eye view" is related to radical insight, the "ah ha" experience that shocks the mind and advances knowledge in new and often unexpected directions.

Having moved beyond the illusion of separateness and, therefore, the need to prove oneself important and distinct from others, Aquarius is concerned with the ideals and aspirations that characterize humanity as a whole. Accordingly, it is predisposed to humanitarianism, altruism, and concern for human rights. Its utopian vision sees all people as brothers and sisters whom, if left alone, will naturally do what is required for the good of society. External control, therefore, is regarded as unnecessary. In fact, it conflicts with the Aquarian ideal of independence. Thus Aquarius will rebel against any form of oppression, and is democratic, radical, and revolutionary in its aims.

The symbol of Aquarius is the image of a man bent down on one knee balancing an upturned urn upon his shoulder. The vessel, it should be noted, is open at both ends. The image signifies the human capacity for channeling universal consciousness, which flows downward from heaven to earth. As always with astrological symbolism, the metaphor is apt. For Aquarius does seem to serve as a vehicle for the expression of cosmic mind. The perspective of Aquarius has shifted to an entirely abstract realm, a dimension of mind observing mind; idea interacts with idea in computer-like fashion until a critical mass is reached and the intellect makes a quantum leap to another level of understanding entirely. Seeing how the whole is a synthesis of many parts, Aquarius appreciates the necessity of all things in the broad process of evolution.

This kind of wholistic thinking is in many respects beyond morality. One might call it transmoral, for morality is built into the sign yet transcended at the same time. As the German poet Rilke put it, "nothing that is human is foreign to me." Having gone beyond an egocentric and moral perspective, the mind has surrendered itself to the whole and thus the individual becomes an open receptacle for the influx and outpouring of universal energies. It is not the individual who acts but the whole which acts through him. Aquarius is beyond choice. Personality has become a vehicle for the irruption of divine wisdom. What is expressed, therefore, may have a quality of revelation to it. It reveals, shocks, startles, awakens, and illumines. Aquarius is the archetype of the *Wise Fool* for it tends to blurt out the truth regardless of how upsetting it may be to others.

Taken as a whole, these various Aquarian themes converge into four interconnected needs: (1) the need for **awakening**, revelation, and enlightenment; (2) the need for **liberation**, emancipation, and breakthrough; (3) the need for change, progress, and reform; and (4) the need for **perspective**, overview, and radical objectivity. Each of these needs presupposes the others; thus, they are interdependent.

Leo and Aquarius as Developmental Stages

In the model I espouse, each zodiacal sign constitutes a developmental stage. To some extent, this is intuitively obvious when we observe that each sign evolves out of the one that precedes it; in so doing, the zodiac symbolizes a natural developmental sequence. Earlier signs are necessarily more simple and primitive than later signs. If each sign signifies a specific drive and capacity, then all signs together represent the psyche as a whole—or what Jung called the *Self*. No sign is more important than any other, for all contribute to the totality of the psyche. Also, each corresponds to a distinct period in the human life cycle, which simply means that the perspective and traits of that sign are most in evidence during specific developmental epochs.

The situation is analogous to the evolutionary stages in the development of the human brain. There is an ancient, basically reptilian brain, which is located at the top of the brain stem and which controls the autonomic nervous system. Encircling it is the old mammalian brain, consisting of the limbic system, which controls human feeling and emotion. Finally, there is the new mammalian brain, or neocortex, which wraps itself around the mammalian brain in a pattern of brain-within-brain. The neocortex is the thinking, reasoning ability that separates *Homo sapiens* from the animal kingdom. These three brains appear to have been successively superimposed upon one another. Each retains rulership over its own dimension of bodily and psychic functions.

Likewise in the zodiac, we have a pattern of sign-within-sign, each evolving out of the one that comes before, each adding something new to the evolving complexity of the psyche, each retaining rulership over its own dimension of bodily and psychic functions, and each corresponding to a specific developmental period.

This idea parallels the principle of psychological epigenisis as formulated by Erik Erikson.[1] According to this principle, all that grows has a ground plan, and from out of this ground plan the parts arise, each part having its time of special ascendancy until all parts have arisen to form a functional whole. Originally applied to biology in relation to phases of embryological development, Erikson's principle postulates that psychological growth proceeds in a similar manner. In fact, the zodiac may be a superior system for differentiating and qualifying these various stages. Just as embryological development progresses from the simple cellular state to the complexity of the organism as a whole, so each sign increases in complexity (by incorporating the qualities of all signs that proceed it) as we move around the zodiacal circle. Similar to Eriksonian formulae, each sign-stage represents a specific task, the completion of which paves the way for the next sign.

In a zodiacal developmental model, Leo would correspond to adolescence, or the period from 12 to 18 years of age. As I have written elsewhere,

> We see this clearly in the adolescent's self-consciousness and egocentricity, in their obsessive concern with appearance, image, popularity, socializing, and courtship behavior, in their trying on of various roles, in their need to be an individual yet accepted by peers, in their need to differentiate from the family matrix and consequent rebellion against parental authority, in their attraction to heroes and role models, in their insistence upon choosing their own values, beliefs, and customs, and in their urgent need for attention and validation.[2]

If separation from the family is supported and the adolescent is encouraged to be his own self, a cheerful confidence develops. However, if there is failure at this stage, it will invariably be reflected in issues of self-image and self-esteem. In short, everything about adolescents, from their primary concerns to their characteristic behaviors, epitomizes the sign of Leo. A description of Leo in the standard astrological text is virtually a description of adolescence.

Aquarius, on the other hand, signifies the retirement years from approximately 68 to 80. At this stage there is a detachment from the external symbols that previously defined one's identity. With career (Capricorn) fading into the background, the playing field is leveled and one achieves a new status that is radically open. There is relative freedom from responsibility during this period, and thus the person can do or be anything. The wisdom of the years has hopefully given one a broad perspective and there is a deeper appreciation for how all things change and are but transitional stages in an eternally unfolding process.

Accordingly, individuals experience greater concern for the future welfare of collective humanity. This is a period characterized by the outspokenness of old age, eccentricity ("crazy" grandpa or grandma), experimentation, and relative independence from consensual morality. Think of Ruth Gordon's character "Maude" in the cult film *Harold & Maude*, for Maude epitomizes the Aquarian stage of life.

The point of this brief excursion into developmental psychology is to establish that Leo and Aquarius constitute separate stages of evolution. While one is not better than the other, they do occur at different places on the developmental continuum. Clearly, the evolutionary thrust is toward Aquarius. The sign is not simply descriptive of old age, however, for it signifies a certain evolutionary phase in the development of human consciousness that can be attained at any age. As will be detailed later, Aquarius represents our capacity for enlightenment and so is consistent with the values, perspectives, and practices that contribute to this end. However, one does not have to wait until old age (or another life) to reap the gifts of Aquarius.

The Nature of Oppositions

To fully appreciate Leo and Aquarius we must compare and contrast their respective perspectives. As with any opposition, Leo and Aquarius form two halves of a larger whole. Integration of both halves bestows certain psychological powers that neither sign possesses by itself. An opposition signifies a relationship of complementary opposites, each sign being the "flip side" of the other;

what one is missing, the other one has. On a personal level, this is often experienced as a "see saw" effect; the individual feels himself pulled in two directions at once. In early stages of development, opposing signs present an appearance of mutually exclusive needs vying for dominance. Circumstances evolving out of this angle result in obvious "either/or" situations, the solution to which can only be achieved by doing "both."

Integrating an opposition creates an emergent property that results from a blending of the two principles. Yet, this emergent property is not predictable at a level of analysis of either sign alone. An emergent property occurs at a higher level of complexity than the parts that compose it. To use a common example, the property of "wetness" does not exist at the level of the hydrogen and oxygen atoms that comprise the molecule we call "water". Wetness has no meaning at the atomic level of description; it "emerges" only at the molecular level.

The situation is similar to what occurs when viewing a stereogram. Stereograms are images on paper that at first appear to be no more than random patterns or dots. However, when you relax your eyes and stare at the dots for a while, a three dimensional image coalesces several inches above the plane of the paper that contains the dots. To see this image depends on one's ability to merge multiple objects into one. By allowing the eyes to relax and blur, the muscles that control the eyes are less likely to fix at the same point that they normally would; thus, images begin to overlap and fuse together. The three dimensional object is an emergent property of the ability to see "in stereo." By loosening one's eye muscles and allowing them to cross and focus on a plane above the paper, a three-dimensional image appears floating in the space between.

Likewise with an opposition, the emergent property is a characterological trait that emerges from an integration of the two signs. To release this quality, the person has to position his consciousness at a point above and between the signs that comprise the opposition. If each sign represents an inner voice with its own agenda, the person has to listen to these voices in stereo; in other words, find a way to express both parts simultaneously. This is being in balance with oneself. If Leo says, "Express yourself," and Aquarius says, "Expect the unexpected," then an emergent quality would be the capacity to express oneself in unexpected ways. Of course, there are many other traits that emerge from an integration of Leo and Aquarius, but this simple example serves to point us in the right direction.

Suffice to say that these opposites exist and that Leo and Aquarius signify them. The task before us is how to integrate them into a whole. But what does *integration* really mean? Integration describes a state wherein certain positive abilities and attributes emerge from a blending of two or more principles. The nature of these qualities enhances the functioning of both sides and allows each principle to more readily satisfy itself. Satisfaction, in other words, is a consequence of both principles operating in a harmonious and complementary way.

Conversely, when two or more principles are not integrated, then the nature of those signs/planets operate in a lower, more primitive, and less satisfactory manner. Satisfaction is less stable in that it quickly reverts to a dissatisfied state. Greater anxiety prevails, and each side sees its opposite as a rival and threat. Rather than trusting that the opposing principle is actually a source of enrichment, satisfactions are perceived as mutually exclusive.

Leo and The Personal Will

Before things can be joined to produce a more complex whole, those parts must be adequately differentiated. It is to this end that we now turn. There are several separate but related themes in the Leo-Aquarius mix that bear further clarification. The most central of these has to do with the notion of identity. Although the Sun is the primary organ of identity-making, its motivating principle is Leo. Likewise, although Uranus is the primary organ for a collective (group) identity, Aquarius is its motivating drive. As we shall see, Leo and Aquarius approach the subject of identity in a complementary yet radically different way.

Previously I defined Leo as the need for self-esteem. All Leonine behaviors can be understood in the context of this basic drive. The need for self-esteem, however, presupposes a self that needs esteem, i.e., an identity. Leo, therefore, is the need for validation of a conceptualized self. I say, "conceptualized" because identity is really a concept about who one *is*; it is a construction that consists of one's self-knowledge and self-understanding in relation to the world. Identity is constituted of what one knows or believes about one's appearance, abilities, attributes, intelligence, beliefs, values, and desires.[3]

The self-concept can be distinguished from the self, or ego, which for purposes of this discussion can be defined as a creative process that includes two components: (1) intentionality, i.e., choice making, and (2) expressiveness—making those choices known to others through verbalization, gesture, play, art, or some other creative act. In short, the ego/self is a process of expressing one's intentions in a manner that creates effects. Hopefully, these effects are positive and evoke approval from others—friends, chums, lovers, teammates, schoolmates, playmates, admirers—which leads to self-esteem. According to Hales, the key to self-esteem is self-efficacy, or confidence in one's ability to achieve desired outcomes.[4] This involves active involvement with others and the effective use of one's self-powers, e.g., we want to win the argument, or the game, or the girl, or the applause of an appreciative audience. This part of us seeks glory and triumph. Leo is all about *will*. How strong is one's will? Can we bring about the outcomes we intend? Can we *win?* Hales explains:

> A sense of self-efficacy comes from the experience of being a causal agent in one's environment. The experience of self-efficacy is a pleasurable one; it is the simple but profound joy of making choices, taking action, creating, or, simply put, causing positive change in our environment.[4]

It is important to recognize that it is precisely one's choices that build and maintain an identity. While this process is complex and invariably involves interactions with others, identity is largely constructed from the choices we make.

As the ruler of Leo, the Sun symbolizes the function of will or volition—the power of choosing. It is the Sun's job to fulfill the need that Leo represents. Every choice contributes to the emerging structure of identity. We may express ourselves by choosing to vote Republican rather than Democratic, or by contributing financially to a pet cause. We might decide to take up a particular sport, play a certain kind of music, and purchase a specific make of car. If someone asks who we are, we might say, "I'm a Democrat, a 49er fan, a Buddhist, an aficionado of classical music, owner of a Mercedes, and a professional astrologer." And if that person criticizes any of these things, we might take it personally *because we are identified with these choices.* From the ego's perspective, our choices define us and constitute our primary means for developing self-esteem.

Attachment and Identification

If choices create identity, identity is maintained by attachment. In fact, identity is more or less synonymous with attachment. We get attached to ideas, to opinions, to values, to things—whatever it is that we have chosen. We intend for our choices to be *good* choices, to produce desirable outcomes, because we feel that our self-esteem hangs in the balance. According to Hales, self-esteem is "the evaluative function of the self-concept."[5] It is the affective—or emotional—experience of the evaluations we customarily make with respect to our personal worth. Given what we know and believe about ourselves, do we feel valuable, significant, worthy? Do we like ourselves? Self-feelings are experienced along a continuum, with pride at one end and self-contempt at the other.

Ideally our choices lead to happiness. The activity of choosing is itself enjoyable, which is why Leo is arguably the most joyful sign of the zodiac. Take away choice and unhappiness follows. Not only do we have a need to be self-determining, but we have an attachment to the fulfillment of our intentions. We want our will to prevail; we want to be happy. This is not attachment as a bond of affection, as when a child attaches to its mother for purposes of security. That would be Taurean. Leonine attachment has to do with identification with a preferred experience.

We may, for example, prefer to experience ourselves as strong rather than weak. Thus, we become attached to the idea, "I am strong." Then if something happens that we are not strong enough to handle, we think "Oh no! I am *not* strong," the ego is deflated, and we suffer. Likewise, if we think Billy Bob should love us but, in fact, he ends up with someone else, we think, "Oh no! I am *not* she who is loved by Billy Bob," and we suffer.

Attachment, in other words, is a consequence of identification with one's intentions. And sooner or later, attachment leads to suffering because invariably something happens that thwarts our will. While choice-making can be immensely pleasurable and lead to such heady states as the joy of victory, it is also associated with the agony of defeat. Intentionality leads to joy only so long as one's intentions are fulfilled. If they are not, then the opposite occurs, suffering!

Aquarius and the Cosmic Will

Now here is where the most interesting choice occurs. We get to choose whether we believe that our choices our thwarted by capricious circumstance or by a Cosmic Will. In virtually every sacred tradition there is postulated a Divine Will whose intentions supercede those of its parts, which, likewise, are also embodiments of will. If human beings have a capacity for will and creativity, it is because they are embodiments of the Creative, the ultimate reality.

From a Leo perspective, it is one's intentions, i.e., what one creates, that come to define who one is. Yet, Aquarius approaches the subject of identity in a complementary yet radically different way. If Leo is personal will, Aquarius is Cosmic Will; if Leo is personal identity, Aquarius is collective identity. To even say, "collective identity," poses a paradox, because consciousness is no longer personal at this level. Whereas Leo represents the need for validation of personal identity, Aquarius signifies the need for awakening to a broader, collective self—a transpersonal self that is defined primarily through its identification with the whole—the cosmos. This larger whole includes humanity, but is more, too; it is the supreme intelligence of the Universe that is immanent in all the parts and processes of Nature.

This is an important point because it means that our personal will is subject to a higher will that works through us. Yet, to the extent that we are attached to the fulfillment of our own intentions, we tend to resist the Cosmic Will. In particular, we resist whatever threatens our identity. The ego does not want change, but to be glorified for the perfect being it is right now! Remember Leo has an aversion to defeat and humiliation. Yet, from an Aquarian perspective, humiliation is a prelude to humility, which is a necessary precondition to enlightenment. In a Universe of constant change, attempts to remain the same are futile and lead to suffering. Aquarius regards motion and change as essential principles of the Universe. Material and psychic phenomena are seen as impermanent and illusory manifestations of interrelated dynamic patterns in the ongoing cosmic dance.

The Aquarian perspective, in short, is one that is consistent with sacred traditions. Recall that Aquarian behavior is motivated by four interrelated needs—**awakening, liberation, change**, and **perspective**. Aquarius represents our capacity to perceive the whole and to awaken to a larger reality, and this awakening liberates us from attachments that impede progress. Critical to this perspective is the realization that change is both necessary and inevitable.

In Buddhist philosophy, the doctrine of impermanence refers to the fact that there are no permanent things to be found anywhere in the Universe. Suzuki states "Buddhists conceive an object as an event and not as a thing or substance."[6] Impermanence implies that the Universe is not composed of "things" that change, but changes which are "thinging"—i.e., the Universe and all its parts are processes of continual becoming and decaying. According to Buddhism, it is precisely our ignorance of this fact, coupled with the desire to resist change and remain the same (attachment), which is the root cause of human suffering. As a Zen master remarked, "Renunciation is not giving up the things of this world, it is accepting that they go away."

In Vedic philosophy, Brahman is both the dynamic behind manifestation and the common denominator of all that is manifested. Individual identity has no ultimate reality precisely because it is subject to continuous change. In a Universe consisting of one eternal existence, all change takes place within the unchangeable and is intimately associated with the revelation of the full nature of Brahman. Thus, change is growth and growth itself the gradual unfolding of ultimate reality through the faculties of living beings.

All of this is vaguely uncomfortable to a solar dominated consciousness. Again, Leo is about personal will and attachment to preferred outcomes. It is difficult for this part of our nature to recognize and accept that human will is an extension of the Cosmic Will and must ultimately subordinate itself to this fact.

The thesis of divine action as the matrix within which all finite actions are situated is essential to the teaching of the great Hindu scripture, the *Bhagavad Gita*. According to the *Gita*, the dynamic of our personal nature is derived from the force and will of Krishna. Human actions are integrated into the plan of the Cosmos itself. The will of the individual, even when completely free, could not act in isolation from the Divine Will, because the individual being and will are included in the Universal Being and Will and depend on the overruling Transcendence.[7]

While the name for the Universal Being may vary from one tradition to another, it is crucial to recognize that such an Intelligence exists. Otherwise, one cannot open to it. To the extent that a person remains unaware of, and thus cannot accommodate to this larger intelligence, she will remain ego-bound and attached to the fulfillment of merely personal intentions. And this, invariably, leads to suffering.

What I am suggesting is that Aquarius symbolizes the Cosmic Mind and is thus our link to a higher intelligence. Like a frequency attuned to the infinite or a portal that opens directly to the Absolute, Aquarius is our capacity to channel the Cosmic Will.

Individuality

If Aquarius is symbolic of our need to open to the Cosmic Will, then why is Aquarius is so often associated with "individuality"? Individuality would seem to reflect concerns about being a separate, distinct, unique individual—just the opposite of identifying with the impersonal, collective self articulated in the previous section.

The key to understanding this apparent contradiction lies in the nature of the Sun Aquarius mix. Many of our key-words for signs derive, wrongly, from observations of individuals who have the Sun *in* a sign. But as I stated earlier, the Sun is going to appropriate the sign to it's own agenda. If the Sun is about individual identity and creative self-expression, this is going to be achieved in a manner described by the nature of the sign that the Sun occupies. If the Sun is in Aquarius, this can manifest as a person who constructs an identity by being different, unusual, unconventional, and so on. The impression is then generated that so called "Aquarians" are individualistic and nonconforming, as if the goal of Aquarius is *to be* an individual. But what we are observing is *Sun* in Aquarius, not Aquarius itself.

When the principle of change (Aquarius) is combined with the principle of creativity (Sun), you naturally get someone who expresses himself in a manner that deviates from the norm, someone who, paradoxically, strives for approval by appearing not to need it. Their pride, in other words, comes from flaunting convention and championing change. However, once the sign is separated from the planet that occupies it, the meaning is clear: Aquarius is about evolution toward a broader, collective definition of self. The Aquarian disregard for approval should not be construed as a quest for individuality, but for collectivity—i.e., for linking the individual will to the Cosmic Will.

Conscious Innocence

The Aquarian symbol of the man on one knee holding an upturned urn upon his shoulder is an apt symbol for the proper relationship of human will to Cosmic Will. The fact that the figure is kneeling suggests the need for humility and deference to the higher power. That the urn is open at both ends signifies being an open vessel for the down pouring of an Intelligence and Will that is superior to the individual.

In her book, *The Philosophy of the I Ching*, Carol Anthony makes this attitude the cornerstone of her life work. "Conscious Innocence", says Anthony, "entails keeping the forces of doubt and fear from our inner view."[8] It requires letting go of attachment to preferred outcomes, for such attachments cause envy, willfulness, and impatience. To the extent that we are attached to our intentions, the ego begins to interject with its demands, its hopes and fears, its pacts and vows, and its resistance to anything that contradicts its own purposes. When the ego (Leo) prevails, we rejoice and "feel good"; yet with every setback we feel miserable.

Conscious innocence is the opposite of conscious purpose. It entails a return to purity of mind wherein the help of the Creative can be received. Such a state is predicated upon acceptance that we cannot know the infinity of things that are being orchestrated by the Divine Will. Like an innocent child willing to be led by a trusted and loved adult, conscious innocence requires faith in the cosmos and a willingness to be acted upon by the higher power. Whereas the ego dictates that events proceed in a straight line toward the goal, conscious innocence enables us to trust in the zigzag path of the Creative. "Life," as the bumper sticker reads, "is what happens to you while you're making other plans."

As stated, the need for awakening is one of the four needs that Aquarius symbolizes. We might also call it the need for enlightenment, or self-realization. Again, different traditions utilize different terms that mean more or less the same thing: *to become whole*. In Buddhist philosophy the underlying conviction is that absolute consciousness is realizable through the systematic annihilation of personal consciousness. A central postulate of Buddhism is that self-consciousness has no real existence in that it is predicated upon an illusion of separateness from actuality. While ultimate reality cannot be defined, the individual can, through the practice of meditation, gradually detach from the illusion of personal existence and move toward a state of unitive consciousness. Self-realization is generally considered to be a life-long endeavor of attempting to dissolve one's identifications with the ego by breaking its attachments to various physical, emotional, and mental states—the goal being to attain that highest state of pure, selfless awareness variously called *nirvana, samadhi,* or *enlightenment.*

In Buddhism, all concepts of self are considered attachments. A self-concept, an identity, is an attachment to an idea of what the self is or should be. Buddhists claim that it is precisely this idea of self-permanence, generated by thoughts that are themselves impermanent, that causes suffering. What we consider to be the self (*sattva*) is merely the sum total of one's thoughts, sensations, desires, memories, perceptions, and beliefs as they arise moment to moment. In other words, the concept of self is a narrative, a stubborn fiction, constructed upon the stage of the mind and then deified like a false god. Identity is nothing more than the moment-to-moment connections that are strung together into a story, which we then hold to, "This is *my* story; this is *me*." The problem is, the story changes; it has no permanence. Realizing this, Trungpa Rinpoche says, "Enlightenment is the ego's greatest disappointment."

Karma and Creativity

While perennial traditions agree that the final and ultimate reason for human existence is unitive knowledge of the divine Ground, the process by which this occurs is a creative one. As Teilhard de Chardin put it, *creation is evolution*. In other words, God embodies creativity and God resides at the deepest core of the individual.

Inherent within the human psyche, therefore, is a capacity for both self- and world-creation. The individual, of course, does not create the whole world, only the one which he or she experiences.

This brings the themes of Leo and Aquarius together, for Leo is creativity but evolution (change) is Aquarius. The opposition between them can be reconciled by seeing that *what* one creates is a catalyst for one's own evolution.

The basis for this idea hinges on the claim that self and world are but two sides of a larger, transcendent Self, the *Atman* that is *Brahman*. Realization of this great truth, however, occurs only by degrees, and is intimately linked to the creative process of action. This is the eastern doctrine of *karma*. Karma has two complementary aspects: (1) as a behavioral pattern (action), and (2) as an environmental event (reaction). The relation between action and reaction is linked through the concept of *creativity*. According to this doctrine, an individual's behavior creates the world that he or she experiences, and it is through this self-created experience that the individual comes gradually to learn that self and world are one.

Karma is related to the Taoist principle of opposition. Every action or thing creates its opposite by definition. For example, who an individual conceives himself to be simultaneously implies who he is *not*. This "not-self" conception is the opposite that is sown through processes of identification, i.e., "I am this but not *that*," soon to be reaped through a process of confrontation with some person or situation that embodies the opposite quality. Growth occurs through the integration of the self-created opposing consequence. The tendency is ever toward balance, or psychic wholeness.

Karma, therefore, is creativity; one's actions create the experienced world. Hindu philosophy teaches that all action ultimately leads to the realization that Atman is Brahman; self and world are ultimately inseparable. The identification with ego (separate-self sense) is transcended in exchange for an identification with the whole of Universal Life. "Man can think of his own life," says Hall, "either as the fulfillment of himself, or as the gradual completion of a greater existence of which he is a part and with which he is indissolvably associated."⁹ Ultimate reality is both within and without; Atman is that condition of Universal Consciousness which resides at the deepest core of the human psyche as well as in every situation the individual may encounter. All human relations occur within the context of the larger Consciousness that subsumes them, and are subordinate to the evolutionary intent of this Consciousness.

This implies that a divine purpose is immanent in the karmic feedback processes that occur between the individual and his environment. Events do not happen randomly, but are the concrete derivatives of psychic patterns originating in the mind of the experiencer. By encountering self as it is symbolically reflected in the guise of external conditions, the individual is afforded the opportunity to correct intrapsychic imbalances that may be generative of interpersonal problems.

Rooted in the illusion of separateness, ego-centered action causes the repeated arising of situations that induce suffering. For the average person, life is an unending accumulation and fruition of actions caused by craving and ignorance. Actions are not futile, however, for karmic feedback can be utilized as a tool for liberation since the suffering it induces will often stimulate breakthroughs to higher levels of spiritual awareness. Such breakthroughs involve the gradual recognition that neither subject nor object is substantial or separate.

In Buddhism, self-consciousness is described as the relation between subject and object. The two terms are relative, one implying the other; the subject cannot exist without the object, and vice versa. An object of consciousness may be either the object of sense or the object of thought. One is external, the other internal. These objects are either accepted, to become part of one's self, or rejected to become part of one's shadow, or not-self. What the Buddhist calls the *sattva*, or self-consciousness, is created by the juxtaposition of self and not-self. Yet, according to Buddhism, neither what humans accept or reject is fundamentally real.

When Buddhists repudiate the existence of an eternally abiding pure ego it is meant that like all other phenomena in the Universe one's personal consciousness is subject to change and therefore transitory. Identity as a separate self has no permanence since consciousness is continually subject to transformation into more inclusive states. When questioned about the ultimate state of consciousness and the means by which it is attained, the Buddha made reference to the mystery of fire: "When all the fuel has been consumed and there is no more fuel and therefore nothing upon which to feed, the fire goes out."[10]

Buddha was referring to the relational aspect of consciousness. The fuel upon which the self feeds is the not-self. When consciousness has expanded to the point where it no longer regards anything as foreign to itself, then separate selfhood is annihilated. Individuality dissolves into unity and self-consciousness is transcended. This point is critical: personal, egoic consciousness can only exist in the relationship between self and not-self, and expands into more complex states through the gradual reconciliation of this division.

Whereas Leo is the motive force behind the exercise of will and gives rise to the separate-self sense, Aquarius symbolizes our motivation for resolution of duality into a collective self wherein we feel identified with humanity at large, i.e., we become whole.

BEING IS BECOMING

Again, the key to resolving the Leo-Aquarius polarity is the same as that which leads to enlightenment: *non-attachment*. This can be defined simply as a willingness to change. The individual strives to remain neutral to the effects of action by cultivating an attitude of non-resistance. By surrendering attachment and performing action in a selfless manner, a person can become free of the binding influence of past karma.[11]

Eastern psychologies, of course, are not the only models that promote liberation. Western psychology focuses on helping individuals develop a proper attitude toward change, too. Psychotherapy clients are encouraged to remain open to new perspectives and to re-examine fundamental assumptions about reality.

Eastern perspectives, however, serve to remind us that an important and valuable corollary to a process of self-change is to recognize that self-actualizing dynamics are embedded within the larger intentionality of Nature. Accordingly, every problem, crisis, and external difficulty that one encounters is the expression of an intelligent change process built into the system. All being is a becoming, i.e., a growth toward wholeness. This suggests that having an intent to change is only half the equation; the other half involves letting go and surrendering to a change process that transcends individual will power.

Note how different this is from a strictly Leonine perspective which glorifies the individual will. The Leo part of us is attached to preferred outcomes. We make choices that hopefully result in the fulfillment of our intentions. We wish to gain approval, validation, and recognition for our good qualities. External approval contributes to a positive self-concept and high self-esteem.

Whereas Leo is concerned with being good, victorious, and special, Aquarius recognizes that on a higher level being is becoming. Thus we cannot afford to become overly identified with anything, neither a self-concept nor an external appraisal. For eventually everything will change. And to the extent that we remain attached to (identified with) specific ideas, experiences, and feelings, we will suffer even when these attachments are to things that are right and good. The only way out of the dilemma is to realize that one is not what one thinks, and that the events one experiences—the triumphs and defeats, the conquests and downfalls—do not ultimately define one.

Hindu scriptures teach that Atman unfolds through degrees of realization (over a series of lifetimes) and slowly blossoms into the full awareness of the individual. Atman emerges from Brahman and implies wholeness as a transcendent self that is the revelation of totality (Brahman). Based upon the direct experience of those who have committed themselves to the realization of such knowledge, this teaching is expressed most succinctly in the "great dictum" of the *Upanisads, Tat tvam asi* ("That art thou"); the Atman, or immanent eternal Self, is one with Brahman, the Absolute Principle of all existence.

This idea is repeated again in the Hermetic doctrine of the macrocosm and the microcosm. According to Huston Smith, the entire body of ancient teachings can be summed up in three important words: *Man mirrors cosmos*.[12] Man is the Universe in miniature; such is the bare statement of the doctrine.

Aurobindo asserts that the process of evolution is inevitable although the individual may resist it by stubbornly clinging to some stage of the process, thereby making it more difficult and painful.[13] The freedom the ego desires, says Aurobindo, is not real freedom since the individual is always subject to the more powerful evolutionary intent of the Absolute. The egoistic notion of free will ignores the facts of Nature at work. Given the reality of evolution and the enormous power that lies behind it, the idea of absolute freedom must be abandoned in order to attain true freedom. The individual must realize that he is essentially one with the Absolute and, therefore, really desires the very process he is fighting.

Limitation is attachment to preferred states, exclusive identifications which invariably generate their opposites (shadow) in external circumstance, thereby giving rise to fear, anxiety, negativity, and all manner of compulsive and destructive behaviors that lead to suffering. By relinquishing the exclusive nature of the individual ego and identifying with the true Self, one's desires become those of the Absolute and one is free to do all that one desires. The paradox is obvious: as one lets go of attachments, then possibilities for success are boundless.

EMERGENT QUALITIES

Earlier I stated that integration of the Leo-Aquarius polarity results in the emergence of certain qualities that neither sign possesses by itself. These qualities necessarily involve paradox, for when two opposite principles are reconciled, a paradox results. A paradox derives from an assertion that is self-contradictory, yet at a higher level of understanding emerges as true.

Consider, for example, the practice of *karma yoga* in Hindu philosophy. Karma yoga has to do with desireless action, or action without concern for the results. But how can one perform an action without desire? Is not desire the basis for all action? The contradiction resolves itself when one realizes that karma yoga refers to an attitude one should assume as a consequence of one's belief in karma and as a strategy for achieving personal growth. Creel explains:

> The principal contemporary discussions reinterpret the doctrine of action by placing emphasis not on action but on attitudes involved in action; action has karmic consequences...only if we are ourselves *bound* to that action by our own attachments; what is called for is not the renunciation of action but renunciation in action, or non-attached action or unselfish action.[14]

The Taoist practice of *wu-wei* parallels the philosophy of non-attachment in Hindu traditions and is similarly paradoxical. Although there is no direct equivalent term in the English language, wu-wei has been variously translated to mean effortless effort, non-interference, non-doing, the secret of action without deeds, or actionless activity. Clearly, these phrases are self-contradictory and thus paradoxical. Taylor clarifies:

> The Taoists...did not mean that one should not act, but that one should be fluid and changing enough to always know how to adjust oneself to circumstances. But how to make circumstances work for us? Through noninterference with the natural course of events.[15]

The *wu-wei* principle is often linked to the element of flowing water, which is yielding and fluid, can penetrate obscure places, and wear down the hardest of substances. To practice wu-wei, one must become fluid like the stream. Taylor continues:

> In adopting the attitude of wu, the realized man thus harmonizes with the stream, sees into its inner meaning, transcending it through noninterference. He blends with it by becoming completely still and so paradoxically transforms consciousness through his inaction.

Wu-wei has been taken to mean "following nature," or allowing nature to "run its course." It is the opposite of control, dominance, or manipulation. The essence of *wu-wei* seems to be an attitude of non-resistance, consciously chosen. Lao Tzu, in the classic *Tao Teh King*, speaks of the "virtue of not striving," and Allan Watts refers to *wu-wei* as the policy of "not forcing." To adopt a policy of non-attachment implies trust in the process of life; a conviction that the reason for existence is to grow beyond present boundaries and limitations. It also implies a willingness to suffer—one of Buddha's central teachings. Rather than resist a given situation, the philosophy of *wu-wei* encourages the individual to welcome it, to embrace it with equanimity.

Allowing a life crisis to have its full impact requires trusting that crises are purposeful expressions of a divine ordering principle in nature. Non-attachment joins the individual to the larger consciousness within which he is embedded, dissolving the divisions that separate self from non-self. The ultimate purpose is to attain *nirvana*, the ecstasy of unitive consciousness. Again we have a paradox: embrace suffering to experience bliss!

When Leo and Aquarius are integrated, therefore, an emergent quality is one's capacity to intend something without attachment to the result. From the perspective of the ego, not all experiences are equally preferable. Some are not consciously intended; yet, with integration of Aquarius, there is an equal willingness to embrace that which is *not* intended. One chooses to allow every experience to have its full impact. Imagine an athlete who is equally willing to experience defeat as victory. He intends to win, and brings the full measure of his ability to the contest, but if he loses then he attends to that experience with the same willingness that he brings to triumph. In other words, one chooses to embrace whatever happens. This does not mean that one transcends suffering entirely, but that one is *willing* to be defeated, surprised, or humbled.

THE OBSERVING SELF

We have seen how Leo and the Sun constitute our means for developing a personal identity, or self-concept. This self-identity is constructed from choices we make and from the meanings we attribute to experience. From childhood on, the feedback we receive from important figures—parents, siblings, grandparents, teachers, coaches, peers, bosses—is utilized to construct a story about the self-world relation. Gradually, we develop a personal narrative or "myth" that tells us who we are and what to expect from life. A person operates within this contracted frame of reference as if she were in a trance. In other words, the constructed self is a kind of auto-hypnotic suggestion, a fictional story authored by the individual's own mind.

Realization of the higher self is an awakening from the trance of personal identity. In fact, the word *Buddha* literally means "one who is awake." While enlightenment is the ultimate goal, this is attained only through a *dis*identification with the objects of thought and sense. All people have a capacity to observe, with detachment, the contents of consciousness as they emerge moment to moment. Deikman calls this capacity the *observing self*.[16] Whatever we notice or conceptualize is merely an object of awareness, not awareness itself.

The observing self is an Aquarian function. Like Aquarius, the observing self operates as pure, choiceless awareness. It is the objective witness, the "watcher on the hills." To witness something is to observe it without judgment. Again, this calls to mind the Aquarian propensity for tolerance, detached perspective, broad overview, and radical objectivity. Whereas Leo signifies the functions of will and identification, Aquarius symbolizes our capacity for witnessing and *dis*identification.

This points up an important distinction between the observer and the observed; the observed has boundaries and can be located spatially and temporally. Even a thought takes up mental space, metaphorically, and has a beginning and an end. While the observing self can be experienced, it can never be objectified because *it is awareness itself*.

Vedanta philosophy distinguishes between *Purusha*, the Witness Soul, and *Prakriti*, all the phenomenon of Nature. Pure awareness, witnessing, requires us to step back from the object of our awareness and objectify it. The most important object to observe is the ego, with its pride, its insistence on being right, and its longing for validation.

By strengthening the observing self our egoistic emotions, thoughts, and impulses become less compelling and we are gradually freed from their control. Instead, we use them as feedback to monitor where we are and how we got there. This is precisely what enables change to occur. One is not controlled by the ego to the extent that one can observe it. In fact, most of psychotherapy is based on separating one's awareness from that which is observed—in other words, disidentifying with the contents of consciousness. We call this free association, introspection, reflection and the like, but the end result is the same: to observe with detached awareness the various emotions, ideas, fantasies, and fears that make up the contents of consciousness.

As the observing self gains increasing clarity and stability, the observed world of the ego—its craving for attention, its presumption of rights and importance, its pursuit of glory and triumph—becomes correspondingly less compelling, less dictatorial and unquestioned.

Again, the integration of Leo and Aquarius entails a paradox. Self-realization is an expanding of identity; yet, this expansion occurs through a disidentification with one's prior identity. This requires letting go of one's personal problems, worries, and concerns. Rather than try to solve them, the goal is to witness them, to watch one's distress, to simply be aware of it without judging it, dramatizing it, analyzing it, or justifying it. Krishnamurti calls this "choiceless awareness."

The intention to not have intentions, to not will or resist change, but to allow evolution to unfold of its own accord, is testimony to the paradox of integrating Leo with Aquarius. As one learns to tolerate and accept what previously was threatening to the self, one's identity expands toward the ultimate goal of wholeness, the *Self*.

ON BEING LED

The process of change is beautifully described in the Chinese Oracle, the *I Ching*, or *Book of Changes*. Throughout the *I Ching*, the reader is counseled to follow the Sage, i.e., to allow oneself to be led by the higher power. There are subtle but continuous warnings to avoid misuse of power and to not allow oneself to act arrogantly or precipitously.

Most often the *I Ching's* advice calls for retreat, holding fast, and not acting until the right moment arrives to move ahead. This right moment, however, occurs only when we have become emotionally detached and able to perceive the inner truth of the situation with clarity. This requires what Anthony calls "inner independence," a rock-like steadiness of purpose and disengagement in the face of all challenges. "The steadiness of purpose," says Anthony, "is to be purposeless."[17] Only by remaining open and modest is one able to engage the power of the Creative in finding a solution to the challenge. More often than not, this solution occurs without one's active interference.

Inner independence is a distinctly Aquarian trait. This is not the independence of Aries, which is the right to act autonomously, but an independence that has as its basis a dependence on the Higher Power. Such dependence enables us to become independent of egoistic concerns for praise, approbation, and endorsement. Yet, this itself requires a Leonine act, a choice. The choice is to will a suspension of disbelief in the power of the Creative to lead us to the Promised Land. "The suspension of disbelief becomes a humble acceptance of whatever is going on as part of the zig-zag workings of the Creative."[18]

Allowing oneself to be led, says Anthony, means waiting until the right moment to act. This occurs only when we are freed from the tyranny of the ego and are able to perceive what is correct. Correct behavior is what contributes to the collective good. Yet, paradoxically this also contributes to the development of self-esteem.

Aquarian Self-Esteem

Hales reminds us there are two separate domains for building self-esteem.[19] First is the competence domain, which is the sense that we are good at something and can compete successfully. Since this contributes to pride and confidence, it is Leonian. The other domain that has major importance for self-esteem is altruism, i.e., unselfish concern for the welfare of others. In this domain, self-esteem involves evaluative judgments based on criteria that stem from the cultural values of one's society. If we act in the collective good, then humanity appreciates us accordingly. As such, altruism is primarily an Aquarian experience. Self-esteem, therefore, derives from two sources: (1) the individual's own self-evaluations, "I'm good at such and such," and (2) the evaluations of society, "he's a good person."

Aquarian virtues of honesty, altruism, and concern for human rights tend to be highly valued in most cultures. Such qualities, *prima facie*, have an inherent "rightness" and "goodness" to them. As such, they contribute to self-esteem in a way that Leo behavior alone cannot. To merely win the game, or the applause, to stand out above the crowd, to establish oneself as superior in a given field, will never be enough by itself to sustain a positive self-image. If one acts solely for one's own aggrandizement, one does not win the admiration of others. In fact, just the opposite occurs: scorn. Conversely, we feel efficacious and receive positive inputs to self-esteem when we achieve in areas that contribute to the collective good.

A substantial amount of social psychological research has shown that people engage in altruistic behavior because it is personally rewarding.[20] Quite simply, it feels good to help others. In many instances, the reward-value of an altruistic act far exceeds the reward that would have been experienced from the achievement of a personal goal. To champion a cause in order to promote the welfare of society may be the most effective way of enhancing self-esteem. For not only does it make us feel good about ourselves, but others, too, will judge us positively for our actions. Social activism, therefore, is a fundamental component of self-esteem. What we do for the good of others is also good for us.

Although Leo and Aquarian domains both contribute to the development of self-esteem, they involve relatively independent evaluations that produce qualitatively different affective experiences. The pride one experiences from self-expression, e.g., being selected for the lead in the school play, is different from the pleasure one derives from contributing to a socially worthwhile cause, e.g., advocating for a legal organization that defends victims of hate crimes. Self-expression and altruism, therefore, can be viewed as independent and somewhat interchangeable sources of self-esteem.

This same point was made by Plato. For Plato, the "good life" was a convergence between self-interest and moral obligation to the community. Personal will and good-will intersect at the Leo-Aquarius junction and constitute an emergent quality of "enlightened self-interest". The "good life" is best attained by being a "good person". At a certain level of development we recognize that our own good and the good of the collective are one and the same.

The Paradox of Final Integration

From the forgoing we can readily see that paradox is at the heart of the Leo-Aquarius integration. For the only way to truly access the gifts of Aquarius is through a Leonine act of will; yet this very act of will is to disengage from the ego and to choose "not my will, God, but thy will be done."

Strictly speaking, one never loses the ego entirely, for this would be like a ship without a rudder. Rather, each person must choose to steer her ship in a direction that is harmony with the winds of change, the breath of the Creative.

Just as the reptilian and mammalian brains co-exist with the cerebral cortex, so the Leo component of the psyche must co-exist with Aquarius. The goal is not to drop the ego, but to gradually build and strengthen the Aquarian dimension. This complements and completes the Leo dimension; it does not replace it.

Summing Up

True inner independence is based on acquiring a cosmic point of view, which enables us to act dispassionately and serve the greater good of the greater whole. Liberated from the tyranny of the ego with its coercive tactics and imperious defenses, we learn to serve the good and the true without coming to harm or losing our dignity.

This, in the end, is what the ego wants anyway—to serve the greater good while still retaining an individual sense of self. The paradox is that to attain what it wants, it must integrate the attitude of its opposite sign, Aquarius. It must not engage in pompous displays of pride at hazards conquered, or cry out with wounded pride when things don't go its way. Instead, it keeps detaching and returning to the path, greeting each change with humble acceptance and reacting to victory and defeat with equal equanimity. It learns, paradoxically, that self-esteem is best gained through doing that which benefits others. It discovers that humility and altruism more effectively win the support of one's fellow man than arrogance and egotism.

And, perhaps most importantly, it learns that the correct way to change the world is to change oneself. Revolution is an inside job that begins and ends with the overthrow of *hubris*—human arrogance. In so doing, the ego is unmasked and the true light of the soul shines through.

There is a Buddhist festival similar to our Mardi Gras where all the participants are required to wear masks. The purpose of the mask is to remind the person that personality is created by the mind; it is, in effect, a mask that hides one's true Self. The

Buddhist would say, "Beneath the mask, original face." The experience of discovering one's true self is analogous to waking up.

This process is recounted in a story about the Buddha who, after his enlightenment, passed a man on the road who was struck by the Buddha's extraordinary radiance and peaceful presence. The man stopped and asked, "My friend, what are you? Are you a celestial being or a god?"

"No," said the Buddha.

"Well then, are you some kind of magician or wizard?" Again the Buddha answered, "No."

"Are you a man?"

"No."

"Well, my friend, then what are you?" The Buddha replied, "I am awake."

Chapter Two

The Hero and The Trickster

ARCHETYPAL FUNCTIONS OF THE SUN AND URANUS

In *Part I* we examined the natural polarity of Leo and Aquarius. Each sign was said to symbolize a set of interrelated psychological needs, corollary behavioral traits, and a distinct developmental stage. Leo's behavioral traits were traced to the need for self-esteem and validation of identity, which is exemplified during the period of adolescence. Conversely, Aquarian traits were related to the need for an objective perspective that awakens the individual to a broader, more inclusive identity, a process best exemplified during the retirement years—approximately 68 to 80.

Each sign was described as the other sign's complementary opposite, with both signs constituting a natural marriage that requires balance and cooperation. The greater the integration between Leo and Aquarius, the higher the functioning of both sides. In other words, each sign can potentially enrich the other. Leo, for example, is associated with intentionality and attachment to preferred outcomes. If carried too far, however, this can lead to hubris and egotism. The antidote is Aquarius, which is associated with non-attachment and openness to the influx of the Cosmic Will.

Integration of the two signs was described as a choice (Leo) to be led by the Higher Power (Aquarius). In so doing, the individual develops humility, remains open to change, and naturally evolves toward wholeness

FUNCTIONS AND ARCHETYPES

Whereas *Part I* established why Leo is the basis for personal will and Aquarius for Cosmic Will, now I would like to extend this idea to their planetary counterparts—the Sun and Uranus. It is difficult to talk about signs without at the same time discussing the planets that rule these signs, for signs and planets constitute motive-action systems. The sign is the motive; the planet is the action. If Leo is the need for self-esteem, the Sun represents a set of psychological functions—intentionality, creativity, play—whose purpose is to satisfy this need. Likewise, if Aquarius signifies our needs for revelation and perspective, then Uranus constitutes those actions—awakening, enlightening, objectifying—that are designed to meet these needs.

A planet, however, not only signifies a set of related psychological functions, but also of archetypes that embody and give expression to the cosmic principle behind these functions. An archetype, in other words, manifests as an image, or metaphor, of one or more psychological processes while also symbolizing an aspect of what Jung called the *collective unconscious*.[21]

According to Jung, the collective unconscious (Universal Psyche) is the matrix within which the human psyche derives its form and substance. As such, it is comprised of various principles—archetypes—that inform and structure human consciousness. Leo symbolizes one set of archetypes, Aquarius another. In this article, we will examine those archetypes that are most relevant to understanding the psychological processes symbolized by the Sun and Uranus.

THE SUN

THE SOLAR FACULTY AND ITS FUNCTIONS

Each planet in astrology represents a psychological faculty, which can be defined as an inherent power or ability to perform a function(s). Since a function is the normal or characteristic *action* of any thing, planets perform various actions, e.g., the Sun signifies willing, creating, performing, playing, and romancing. As stated in Part I, solar activities are geared toward satisfying a set of interrelated needs symbolized by Leo. These include (1) the need for validation, approval, and attention, all of which contribute to **self-esteem**—the primary motive; and (2) the need for play, creativity, and **self-expression**, which is the secondary motive.

As the active agent of these needs, the Sun represents a specific psychological faculty. While there is no single term within psychology that correlates to the various functions of the Sun, the most equivalent term would be the ego, or self. For our purposes, the solar ego/self can be defined as a psychological faculty that includes six interrelated functions.

1. **Intention** (will, volition, choice). The ego, in other words, is our capacity *to intend* something.

2. **Creative self-expression**, or simply *creativity*. This is our ability to bring something into being that did not previously exist. The Sun, therefore, is the primary organ for creating the reality which one experiences.

3. **Identification.** Human beings have a tendency *to identify* with various internal and external phenomena, e.g., subjective qualities like strength or beauty, and objective conditions

like occupation, race, and nationality. Identifications *create* identities.

4. **Performance.** Individuals have the capacity to act, perform roles, and express themselves in ways that are designed to amuse and gain attention. The capacity to attract attention is a primary contributor to self-esteem.

5. **Play and Recreation.** The ability to occupy oneself in amusement, sport, or other recreation. Play is essential for self-enjoyment, as when one *plays* a game or an instrument, or performs in a "play".

6. **Courtship and Romance.** Courtship is an attempt to gain the favor of someone through attention, praise, or flattery. Romance signifies a high level of ardent emotional attachment to the object of one's attention.

Note that each solar function is closely related to all the others, which is why they constitute a set. The most basic of these functions is **intentionality.** This can simply mean directing one's attention to something. Yet, the choice to selectively attend to one thing and not another is itself an act of **creativity,** for by one's attentions one brings into focus a world.

The tendency **to identify** with one's choices, e.g., to choose to play the clarinet but not the violin, is conducive to creating an identity, as "I am a clarinet player." One may also choose to express oneself in a manner designed to amuse and gain attention, i.e., **perform,** thus further contributing to a positive identity, or self-esteem.

To the extent that one has self-esteem, there is a corollary capacity to enjoy oneself through various forms of **play and recreation.**

Self-esteem enables one to contribute to the self-esteem of others by expressing praise, attention, or flattery, which are the core actions involved in **courtship.**

Thus we find that each solar function is inseparably intertwined with every other. The end product of this braid of actions is the goal of the entire solar process: the construction of a personal identity and its affective component, self-esteem.

THE EGO

Western psychology regards the self as a type of object that is localized in the body and separate from other objects, the "skin encapsulated ego," as Allan Watts called it. Boundaries are essential to the formation and maintenance of a personal identity. The ego boundary is akin to a surface of tension that operates like a semi-permeable membrane between the conscious and unconscious portions of the psyche, as well as between the individual and his or her outer surroundings. Thus defined, the ego becomes a segregated system within the psyche and within the external environment. Although it has a boundary, this boundary is not fixed, but expands by including new things—e.g., new possessions, friends, abilities, ideas, values—and contracts by excluding things. Generally speaking, inside the boundary would be all things with which the individual felt identified; outside would be everything from which the individual feels alienated, hence producing feelings of disinterest, indifference, fear, suspicion, and aversion.

As the conscious, self-aware portion of the personality, the ego courts approval from others by excluding from awareness those thoughts, feelings, and impulses that it perceives as threatening to the current regime. Because the ego contains a large measure of self-deception, it is believed to be the object of self-love and ego-defense. Devoted primarily to the continued maintenance and glory of itself, the ego will instinctively suppress anything that seems to threaten its survival—not physical survival, but survival of one's identity and self-esteem.

The initial goal of the ego is differentiation of a self from the environment. I say *a* self rather than *the* self, for as has be shown, one's self-concept is an arbitrary, constructed entity that has no real permanence, i.e., is subject to change. Once a self is constructed, other people are divided into two categories: those that enhance and those that diminish one's self-esteem. In other words, from the perspective of the ego, the social environment is reduced to an audience of potential admirers or detractors. The value of others is determined on the basis of whether they are worthy of identification, i.e., the ego asks, "Are they like me, or unlike me?"

The ego/self is necessary for psychological as well as physical survival. Indeed, failure to establish a sense of one's own boundaries leads to retarded development and even psychosis. Without a strong, bounded sense of self, the individual is prone to excessive dependence on others for approval and self-esteem, is compelled to comply with environmental demands, suffers a preoccupation with "image" and appearance, is extremely vulnerable to failure and humiliation, experiences chronic feelings of worthlessness, and may be afflicted with an underlying sadness and loneliness.

Like a castle's walls that keep what is valuable safe from intruders, the ego assures that one's self-interest is defended. Ego boundaries are also necessary to keep from being overwhelmed by contents that stream in from the collective dimensions of the psyche. Mozart, for example, was inspired by music that seemed to be channeled from a Neptunian dimension (Sun opposition Neptune), yet was unable to manage his health and finances and died early. History is littered with talented individuals who were burnt out and destroyed by transpersonal energies they could not contain.

It is easy to disparage the ego and blame it for all our problems.

For it can be a source of vanity, susceptible to envy, demanding of special treatment, vindictive when slighted, unable to admit wrongdoing, narrow, selfish, and so on. Yet, it is important to recognize that there is nothing intrinsically bad or negative about the ego. It has its proper and necessary role to play in the psychic compound. Without a strong ego, one has no sense of identity, no purpose, and is thus buffeted about by the vagaries of apparent chance. The ego gives us the capacity to choose, to will. It also enables us to validate and encourage the will of another—which is to love in a romantic sense. Without a sense of identity and purpose, there is little justification for living. The ego is our rudder in the stormy seas of life. It is our steering mechanism, the helmsman that guides the ship of fate. For behind every fated circumstance is a choice once made.

Within its own domain, and expressed in a balanced way, the ego is a beautiful and glorious thing. It is the intrepid Hero and Heroine, the stunning entertainer, brilliant performer, triumphant conqueror, royal majesty of king or queen, the jubilant victor, brave champion, and immortal beloved. We enjoy seeing it, feeling it, and expressing it. We identify with actors and actresses that embody qualities of confidence, strength, and joy, and with sports heroes who show us how to win. After all, this is how we want to be. We can no more lose our egos than our hearts. What we can do is purify the ego of its gross elements and more extreme manifestations—it's overweening pride, self-aggrandizement, insincerity, and glory-seeking.

The Constructed Self

A first step in liberating oneself from the ego's excesses is to recognize that the ego and the self-concept are not the same thing. Just as there is a difference between a manufacturing process and its product, e.g., an automotive assembly line and the auto itself, so there is a difference between the ego and its product, personal identity. The ego is a series of actions—choosing, attending, identifying, creating, playing—but the end result of this solar assembly line is an organized system of ideas that constitute the self-concept.

As the individual experiences the consequences of his self-expression, ideas form and decisions are made as to what constitutes good or bad behavior. Most of us don't realize that identity is created by a loose backdrop of concepts, values, and roles that are arbitrarily chosen. Once chosen, they harden into a reality orientation that defines who we perceive ourselves to be. This reality, however, is severely contracted and excludes possibilities for alternative identities. It is, in effect, a personal myth—a story.

Just as actors assume roles/identities and act "as if" they are that person, so individuals assume roles and act "as if" they are limited to a specific role in a personal drama. This "as if" quality is evident in the roles that are assigned to us by culture, religion, parents, profession, and so on, without our realizing their arbitrary, constructed quality. They are scripts, fictions into which we pour our souls.

Personal identity is a trance that, at least for the first half of life, is absolutely necessary. Once established, however, the self does not give up control and will dominate consciousness unless challenged. After all, one's self-concept is the product of a strategy designed to assure approval and avoid disapproval. It develops through relationships with significant others, beginning with one's parents. Yet, these constructed self-images are merely ideas that have taken hold of the person, like a false king that has temporarily dethroned the true leader of the personality—the *Self*.

According to Jung, the Self transcends and encompasses the ego. As an expression of psychic wholeness, it includes conscious and unconscious contents, and is both the center and circumference of the psyche. The ego-self, by comparison, is a limited, ephemeral thing, a petty tyrant that is self-perpetuating and operates as a kind of organized pride system that protects the person from embarrassment and disappointment. Once created, however, the ego tends to assert that it really is the glorious being it pretends to be.

As stated, there are six main functions that are signified by the Sun. Let us now examine three of these functions more closely—intentionality, creativity, and identification—and, in so doing, identify the archetypes that symbolize them.

INTENTIONALITY

The first place to start in our analysis of will is to recognize what will is not. It was Freud's great contribution to point out that the will is not the prime mover of the psyche; rather, we are influenced by a host of unconscious urges, wishes, fantasies, and desires that fuel the engine of the mind. We might decide this or that, but before we do we will have had to juggle a throng of drives that press for fulfillment. Like a group of unruly knights and nobles in feudal Europe, each planet in astrology has its own agenda, its own purpose, while it is the Sun's job to rule over its subjects. In other words, the Sun must conquer and subjugate the warring elements of the psyche and make them subservient to a rational agenda.

Intentionality, says Rollo May, "is the capacity to have intentions."[22] But an intention is the blossoming of a psychic process that stems from myriad subsystems, each of which has its own intentions. *To will* is to make a conscious choice. It is not an impulsive, spontaneous act. Intention wells up from deep within and requires an effort of sustained openness to whatever cues may flow from one's body and feelings. The planets have their own voices, which we experience as feelings. Mars says, "do it now!" while Saturn says, "be patient."

Again, the image of the king ruling over his subjects comes to mind, for the Sun must direct a diffuse array of wants and needs, information and interests, hopes and fears, in short, our whole being (inner kingdom). Small wonder that a paralysis of will so often plagues the individual. Much of the time our attention is spread over a variety of intentions, some consonant, some diverse, or even contradictory. It is easy to see this in the astrological chart with its lines of tension symbolized by planetary aspects. If the chart could speak, we would hear a rich medley of voices, or perhaps a cacophony. What is to bring order out of this chaos of incipient action? Our answer is *the Sun*.

What we call will, or intentionality, is actually a series of operations that culminate in action. William James pointed out that preceding will is *attention*; we first attend to something, bring it into focus, and then decide what to do. Among the many sensations and stimuli affecting us, we have the power to throw our weight on this possibility rather than that. We say in effect, "Let *this* be the reality for me." This fiat, "Be it so!" is the Jamesian statement of what is today called commitment. Attention, therefore, is an intention, a choice to attend to one thing rather than another.

Another component of will is *wish*. Once we give our attention to an imagined possibility, we may wish for it to be realized. We play with the possibility in our minds, so to speak, before committing to the requisite action. As May defines it, wishing is the capacity to imagine a fulfillment and is a necessary beginning element that sets every act of will in motion. If I say, "I wish I could buy that house," the wish provides the fuel for a potential action. If I believe that what I wish for is within my power, and there is sufficient absence of conflict, then I *will* buy that house.

A third component of will is *meaning*. The existentialist philosophers—Brentano, Heidegger, and Husserl—made much of this idea, namely that consciousness never exists in a vacuum but always is consciousness *of* something. To attend to this something, whether a subjective feeling or an external object, is to simultaneously give it a meaning. If I feel tense and heated, I may interpret this to mean, "I'm angry." If I notice a woman look away as I direct my attention to her, I may interpret this to mean, "She's not attracted to me". Yet, by these meanings I am creating my experience as much as I am observing it. Meanings are not given, but created. In this way, attention and meaning co-construct reality.*

An "intent" is the turning of the mind toward an object, which has a certain import or meaning. I intend to climb a mountain *because* it poses a challenge. That is its meaning for *me*. Intention always implies a meaning about the thing intended. This meaning, moreover, is a creative act; it serves to shape the world as much as the world shapes us. One person looks at a mountain and sees a majestic image that inspires the impulse to paint. Another sees it as a place to vacation, another as a challenge to climb. The meaning of the mountain, therefore, is inseparable from the intention of the observer—to paint, vacation, or climb. Each intention will evoke different fantasies and feelings, i.e., a different experience. Thus the meaning of an object and our intention toward it are reciprocal. Intention contains both our knowing and our creating reality.

The final component of will is *action.* It matters little to intend something if one does not do what one intends. This is simple enough. Yet, very often we lack the will to face something because it arouses too much anxiety. We can't "handle" it, e.g., a therapy client cannot remember something from childhood that was

---

* Meaning in this sense is not the same as the Sagittarian quest for meaning. Sagittarius symbolizes the need to discover the meaning of something for itself, e.g., the meaning of life, of a biblical passage, or of an astrological configuration. This is a transpersonal, philosophical approach to meaning, as in formulating a hypothesis, constructing a theory, or deducing a purpose.

traumatic. Until the client feels safe, and is encouraged by acceptance, she cannot bring herself to take a stand toward what scares her.

The capacity to have intentions varies tremendously from person to person, and it is the Sun's sign, house, and aspects that reflect this capacity. For example, I had a client with Sun in Capricorn forming a closing square to Saturn in Aries, within one degree of exactitude. She complained that she lacked discipline, was disorganized, and put things off to the last minute. As a consequence of her procrastination, she was constantly stressed by unfinished tasks and suffered from insomnia.

As a child, her father was extremely critical, judgmental, and scolding. A harsh disciplinarian, he threatened her with constant pressure. The only way my client could protect her self-esteem (Sun), was to discredit her attacker (Saturn/father). Her defense was simple: don't pay attention to him. This intention to not attend, however, also extended to her relationship with her internal Saturn. Thus, every time she heard its voice, "plan your day, balance your checkbook, discipline yourself to spend wisely," she ignored it. She *wished* to get organized, but could not follow through with the requisite action; thus her intention was aborted. To actually be organized meant she had to face her Saturn, which she could not do. So she put it off, as it to say, "No, you can't hurt me anymore; I won't let you."

Note in the above example there are two conflicting intentions: (1) the unconscious intention to not attend to Saturn, and (2) the conscious intention to attend. In disorders of will, there is often a paralyzing ambivalence that stems from unconscious conflict of this sort. My client did not know she had an unconscious intention to ignore Saturn's voice in the same way that she ignored her father (after high school she did not talk to him for seven years). Different planets in hard aspect to the Sun can compromise our intentions in different ways. In each instance, there are conflicting needs that vie for dominance.

The Sun/Leo's need, of course, is for self-expression and self-esteem. Given sufficient pressure from an outer planet, however, and the relatively simple act of being a person, of having worth, of winning accolades and triumphing over one's fellows, can arouse the most debilitating guilt. One might believe at an unconscious level that s/he is undeserving of good fortune due to imaginary crimes committed in childhood. Or s/he could fear that self-esteem and happiness are of such limited quantity that whatever s/he enjoys of it will deprive others. The list goes on; suffice to say here that anxiety and guilt are enemies of intentionality.

There are many of us who are so detached and alienated from our own experience that we cannot will anything. Detachment (Uranus) is the opposite pole of intentionality. If I distance myself from my inner experience to the extent that I am cut off from my own urges, feelings, and sensations, then I cannot be authentic; I cannot be real because I am not in touch with my own reality. If I merely intellectualize about my wishes and needs yet cannot act because of unconscious conflict, then I emasculate any possible intention that may arise. One must "take a stand" in relation to one's experience, or it cannot lead anywhere

THE RULER ARCHETYPE

This capacity to take a stand—to intend—is associated with the **Ruler** archetype. In many myths, fairy tales, and legends, the main character discovers at some point that s/he is really the long-lost son or daughter of the King.

A good example of this is the Alexandre Dumas novel, *The Man In The Iron Mask*, which was recently made into a movie starring Leonardo DiCaprio. The adventure begins deep inside the Bastille, where a twenty-three-year-old prisoner named "Philippe" has languished for eight long years, unaware of his true identity or what crime he has committed. As the story unfolds, we discover that he is actually the twin brother of the selfish, arrogant King Louis XIV.

By the end of the story, Philippe, with the help of the Three Musketeers, has "taken a stand" and assumed his rightful place as the King of France, displacing his cruel, despicable brother. Phillipe's ordeal of living in poverty and subsequent imprisonment helped him to develop the humility and empathy necessary to great leadership. Such stories symbolize how we all must discover our intrinsic royalty, shed our hubris, and demonstrate a capacity to rule over our own, inner kingdoms.

When the archetype of the Ruler is functioning in a healthy, integrated way, the person assumes complete responsibility for his life—not only for his inner reality, but also for the way his outer experience mirrors that reality. For example, if our kingdoms are barren, this reflects some barrenness within ourselves. This is consonant with the idea that our intentions mold the shape of the world we experience; i.e., experience tends to conform to our intentions, both conscious and unconscious.

When the ruler archetype is functioning properly, we enjoy life and have confidence in our ability to make something of ourselves. An ability to create a positive identity and lead a meaningful life is the primary function of the Sun. A strong Ruler enables one to be sovereign in one's kingdom and to make life the way one wants it to be.

"The Ruler," says Pearson, "creates a peaceful and harmonious kingdom by becoming peaceful and harmonious inside."[23] This necessitates that the individual stay attuned to his subordinates—the planets—allowing each to have its own voice. A good Ruler (Sun) does not ignore his inner promptings, or attempt to suppress them, but remains sensitive to the needs of each and every part of his inner kingdom. If there are conflicts, an effective ruler will negotiate a truce and affect compromises that allow for internal unity and peace.

The Ruler has responsibility for delegating responsibility to the appropriate experts—the planets—each of whom is in charge of a singular aspect of the kingdom. In this regard, the fully actualized Ruler is really the *Self* in Jungian terms, i.e., the totality of the psyche under rulership of a divine ordering principle. Astrologically, we are not Suns but solar systems—Sun *with* planets. This means it is the Sun's job, as ego, to integrate and bring into balance the whole of the psyche and thus to actualize the Self.

Just as all good monarchs identify with the good of the collective, balancing personal aspirations with other people's needs, so, too, each person must expand his identity to encompass a larger sphere. Each person must act to create the life she wants, but also keep in mind what is good for society. Otherwise, one falls prey to what Pearson calls "the Shadow Ruler," the dark side of egoic power. To the extent that the individual is cut off from his own insides, and especially from those dimensions of the psyche that are symbolized by the outer planets, he develops into a lop-sided, one-dimensional caricature of the Ruler archetype, an ogre tyrant so consumed by personal needs for glory and triumph that he is oblivious to the impact his decisions have on other people.

The Shadow Ruler operates like his kingdom is under attack, which it may well be, for the suppressed elements of the psyche inevitably revolt. He then acts with the desperation, narrow-mindedness, and vindictiveness of a besieged despot—in a word, s/he is *defensive*. Again, a good example of the Shadow Ruler was portrayed by Leonardo DiCaprio in his portrayal of young Louis XIV in *The Man In The Iron Mask*.*

---

* DiCaprio played both roles—Philippe who had been imprisoned in the Bastille, and his cruel twin brother, Louis, who had usurped the throne.

CREATIVE SELF-EXPRESSION

The second function of the Sun is *creativity*. "In the beginning God created." Those first words of the Bible characterize the primary attribute of the Divine as the ability to create. In his book, *Creative Evolution,* Henri Bergson pointed out that creativity was not simply in a being transcendent to Nature, but the very stuff of nature itself. Similarly, Alfred North Whitehead asserted that creativity is the ultimate reality of which all things are instances.[24] His was a doctrine of permanent and immanent creation; that is, the self-creation of Nature. "Creativity is...the ultimate reality, which is embodied in all individuals, from God to electrons," says David Ray Griffin.[25]

Creativity can be defined as the ability to bring into being something that did not previously exist. Normally we think of creativity in the sense of an artist who produces a work—a sculpture, painting, or song. But this is a conservative, limited description of creativity. If God is equivalent to creativity, and human beings are embodiments of the divine, then perhaps we, too, have the ability to create worlds.

A broader definition of creativity would be "the ability to generate conditions through intentions." This, of course, is precisely what is meant by the eastern doctrine of karma. The popular usage of the word karma in Western culture has come to be understood as equivalent to fate and associated with forces beyond human control. In its pure sense, however, karma simply refers to action (*karman*). Every action leaves its residue (*samskara*) in the memory of the person, and these residues collectively form habit patterns (*vasana*) that dictate personality. The roots of karma, therefore, are in what modern psychologists would call *beliefs* or *cognitive structures.* The process is self-sustaining in that action creates memory, memory coalesces into guiding beliefs, and beliefs determine further actions. Psychologically, it is a closed, self-perpetuating loop.

Entering into this loop, however, and becoming part of it, are the environmental consequences of actions. Habitual actions function like seeds, impregnating the world with the essence of one's being. These seeds become one's fate, ripening when the time is right. It is one's actions alone that make up the code of fate. The seed produced bears the same structure as the one who produced it; thus, the conditions which result will mirror the psychic structure of the person who produced the original seed. As within, so without. Action and event, psyche and environment, have the same or similar quality. In a word, they are *isomorphic*.

It is for this reason that Chapple emphasizes that karma is creativity; one's actions create the experienced world.[26] This, of course, is a much broader definition of creativity than one that depicts it as merely the ability to produce artifacts. From a karmic perspective, the reifying process of the mind tends to create the very conditions it observes. This is not idealism in the sense that reality is a purely subjective invention. For it recognizes that the external world is real, but not ultimately real; it is a product not simply of perception, but of the creative powers of the mind itself. In this view, concrete worldly experience is generated by one's intentions, both conscious and unconscious.

Of course, one hopes that one's intentions produce desirable outcomes that lead to self-esteem. This, after all, is the Sun's goal. Yet, to the extent that one is not well integrated, renegade forces within the psyche will subvert the intentions of the ego. When problems arise, the healthy individual is willing to see them as manifestations of disharmonious forces within the psyche, and as opportunities for self-correction.

THE CREATOR ARCHETYPE

The archetype that corresponds to the solar function of creativity is clearly the *Creator*. Pearson points out, however, that it is our Souls, not our egos that create our lives. "When we become aware of our connection with the creative source of the Universe, we also begin to become aware of our part in creation."[27] In other words, our capacity to create derives from the deepest, most interior part of ourselves; the Creator is our divinity within, or what Jung would call the *Self*. Again, this involves the Sun and all the planets, too. The Creator archetype is evident in all creation myths. Whether we call it God, Brahman, Tao, or any other name, the Creator is the divine source of the Universe. What is critical for each person to realize is that this archetype is immanent within human consciousness as well.

I believe one's intentions mobilize the creative potency of the higher power, enabling us to borrow this power, as it were, for our own purposes. However, if we are not creating consciously, so that it seems that we are products of our environment—the created—rather than of ourselves, then we are in the grip of the shadow Creator: creating without any sense of responsibility for what we are making. I realize it is a common new-age platitude to say, "Well, s/he created that". Too often this response merely substitutes for authentic compassion and is a way of distancing oneself from another's suffering. Yet, I also believe it is a mistake to assume that somehow we are victims of a capricious Universe that, without purpose or reason, afflicts us with pain.

While it is critical to not identify with our suffering, i.e., not assume that a bad experience means we are bad people, it is important to embrace every experience with the conviction that somehow it is meaningful, and it has been earned. We earn it simply by virtue of being human, which makes us imperfect and incomplete. Pain, as Kahil Gibran writes, "Is the breaking of the shell that encloses your understanding....It is the bitter potion by which the physician within you heals your sick self."[28]

Once we give up the illusion that we can control our destiny strictly by an act of will, then we begin learning to trust the ways in which our Souls are creating our lives. Though the *Self* is notorious for its lack of concern for ego success, it is seeking our growth and development on a deeper level.

Jung claims that with every conscious choice we arouse a response in the unconscious, which compensates our conscious intentions in order to bring about balance and wholeness. This is similar to the idea of karma, which postulates that every action produces an equal and opposite reaction. Jung was simply saying that this tendency toward balance and wholeness occurs internally as well as externally.

Accordingly, to the extent that we identify with the whole of ourselves, both conscious and unconscious, then we have the experience of choosing everything that happens. Can you imagine that? No matter what happens, to say "I *choose* this"? I choose *this* divorce, *this* cancer, *this* death.* Such an experience requires that we identify not with our ego, but with our Soul. It requires obeisance to the Cosmic Will that is orchestrating the infinity of things within and without that are necessary for the greater good of the whole, and which may at times necessitate frustration of our individual pursuits. This perspective, of course, is the Uranian counterpart to the Solar Ego—a point we will return to later.

---

* This does not obviate a counter-choice to act in accord with a preferred reality, e.g., one can choose to recover from cancer. However, when such a choice acts in concert with (rather than opposed to) the prevailing reality, there is less struggle, fear, and conflict, which paradoxically allows one's efforts to be in synch with a higher power and thus more likely to succeed. This is precisely what it means to be 'cool under pressure' and to balance intentionality with a healthy detachment to any particular outcome.

Identification

A third solar function is that of *identification.* One might not think of this process as a verb—a tangible action. Yet, identification is inescapably a consequence of our intentions. Every choice I make is governed by something in me which prefers that experience over another. I chose the college I wanted to attend, the woman I wanted to marry, the car I wanted to drive—because they reflected my values, preferences, and desires. They are the objects in which I invest my self-esteem; e.g., I want my college to be a good college, my wife to be lovely, my car to be reliable, and so on.

Identification is the process by which we develop an identity. May points out that Descartes was wrong in his famous sentence, "I think, therefore, I am." For this formula leaves out exactly the variable that is most significant, *will.* It would be more accurate to say, "I will, therefore, I am." According to May, "It is in intentionality and will that the human being experiences his identity."[29] If we intend to vote Democratic, cheer for the Yankees, and practice astrology—these are intentions around which we define ourselves, i.e., we identify with democrats, Yankees, and astrologers. Our choices are like bricks in the structure of identity. And lest we forget, our choices are free. Identity is not given, it is constructed.

The Hero Archetype

The archetype that fundamentally has to do with processes of identification is the Hero. The most celebrated archetype in myth and literature, the Hero symbolizes the ego and what it hopes to achieve—an identity that is virtuous and true. More precisely, the Hero is the ego-ideal—the best we can hope to become. In Joseph Campbell's landmark work, *The Hero with a Thousand Faces,* he asserts that the most persistent theme in oral tradition and recorded literature is the myth of the Hero.* The Hero's story, says Campbell, is essentially a symbolic journey that reflects the soul's search for wholeness. During the journey the Hero encounters all manner of different archetypes—warriors, monsters, helpers, demons, servants, scapegoats, masters, seducers, tricksters, lovers, friends, and foes. Yet, each archetype is a facet of the Hero's own true self.

Following the tradition of Carl Jung, Campbell believes that the psyche is divided into archetypal characters that symbolize different psychological functions. While each archetype has its part to play in the life story, it is the task of every human being to integrate these parts into a unified whole. The ego (Hero) initially thinks it is separate from its parts, yet it must incorporate them, i.e., identify with them, to become the *Self*—a complete, balanced, integrated human being capable of expressing all the archetypes. This, in effect, is the Hero's journey.

It would seem that the Hero's journey is best symbolized by the Sun. The Sun is the ego, the archetype of the Hero, and is on a journey toward becoming the Self—the archetype of wholeness. According to Jung, the Self incorporates within its paradoxical unity all the opposites embodied in the various archetypes. Astrologically, this means integrating the polarized sign-pairs of the zodiac and their respective ruling planets into a unified whole. With a central Sun surrounded by planets, the solar system is an apt symbol for the Self, which Jung defined as the center and circumference of the psyche. The process of individuation that leads to realization of the Self is the Hero's journey. This means that the person must identify with each and every part of his psyche. The ego must incorporate all the planets and their respective functions into a new, unified whole.

---

* I use the word Hero to describe a central character or protagonist of either sex.

Ultimately, a Hero transcends the bounds and illusions of the ego, but at first, Heroes are all ego—the I, the one, an individual separate from the rest of the group. Whatever forms the Hero takes, the story is essentially the same: the Hero and the kingdom are in danger from some hostile force; something needs to be rescued, both inside the self as well as in the world beyond. An inner conflict is balanced by an outer conflict. The key to saving the kingdom—both inner and outer—is having the courage to face whatever is threatening the integrity of the system, which is generally some rejected part of one's own soul—the shadow—as symbolized by a condition of evil in the outer world. The Hero must defend the gates and protect the boundaries of the kingdom so that life within can flourish and grow. But this means facing and vanquishing the shadow.

Being a Hero is about making the right choices and doing the right thing. But there are many right ways to be, and the Hero must find a way to be them all, in the right proportion, and at the right time. To appreciate the difficulty of this, one has only to remember the woman with Sun square Saturn who could not allow herself to be saturnine—i.e., organized, disciplined, focused, and responsible. Saturn was an enemy in her own mind. It wasn't just her father with whom she was at war, it was with the Saturn in herself. Yet, to be a truly noble Heroine, worthy of esteem and respect, she must make an ally of all the figures and characters that reside within her kingdom. To the extent that she fails at this, the externalized version of her rejected part(s) will dishonor her, e.g., Saturn will subvert her intentions and she will suffer loss of esteem.*

It is the job of the ego to create boundaries—a separate self—that houses the Soul and enables it to evolve over time. Without a

---

* I am not saying here that Saturn is the shadow in an archetypal sense, for that role belongs more properly to Pluto. However, any planet can be thrown into shadow given the right combination of factors (aspects and house position).

well-built container, there can be no real psychological or spiritual development because there is no safe place for it to occur. A confrontation with the unconscious or with the transpersonal can crack an inadequately developed ego and result in psychosis. In addition to creating boundaries, however, the ego must integrate the shadow and thereby expand the boundaries of identity. In so doing, the Hero's personality is restored to unity. The missing piece may be a critical psychological function such as the ability to love or trust—or, Heroes may have to overcome a problem such as lack of patience or decisiveness. Once the shadow is integrated, the achievement of wholeness is symbolized by the Hero's initiation into a larger group or world.

People commonly think of Heroes as strong and brave, but these qualities are secondary to **sacrifice**—the true mark of the Hero, according to Campbell. Sacrifice is the Hero's willingness to *give up an attachment,* perhaps even her own life, on behalf of an ideal or a group (Aquarius). They may give up a loved one or friend along the way. They may give up some cherished vice or eccentricity as the price of entering into a new way of life. They may return some of their winnings, or share what they have gained of their journey. They may return to their starting point, the tribe or village, and bring back boons, elixirs, food, or knowledge to share with the rest of the group.

Sacrifice here has two meanings: (1) the willingness to give-up an attachment, i.e., an identification with something that circumscribes and limits the self; and (2) a willingness to act on behalf of the group rather than oneself. In other words, one gives up an attachment in order to identify with a larger, collective self and thus act for a greater cause. The Hero is about taking a journey to find the treasure of one's true self and then returning home with a gift that transforms the kingdom and, in the process, one's own life.

Uranus/Aquarius, of course, symbolizes everything that the Hero must become—whole, humane, non-attached, able to see the big picture, dedicated to the group, and so on. In effect, the true Hero represents an integration of the Leo-Aquarius axis. This was exemplified in sterling fashion by that arch-Aquarian, Spock, when he gave up his life to save the crew of the Enterprise in *Star Trek II*. Captain Kirk cried out in anguish, "Why, Spock, *why?*" Spock responded without hesitation, "The needs of the many outweigh the needs of the one." Film reviewer Roger Ebert comments:

> The peculiar thing about Spock is that, being half human and half Vulcan and therefore possessing about half the usual quota of human emotions, he consistently, if dispassionately, behaves as if he possessed very heroic human emotions indeed. He makes a choice in *Star Trek II* that would be made only by a hero, a fool, or a Vulcan. And when he makes his decision, the movie rises to one of its best scenes.[30]

In effect, Spock decides to be a Hero, which means he is more identified with the group than he is with his solitary self. This capacity for an altruistic act that evidences concern for the future welfare of the human race is the hallmark of Aquarius. As the sign opposed to Leo, Aquarius signifies the completion and culmination of the Hero's Journey.

URANUS

THE URANIAN FACULTY AND ITS FUNCTIONS

Just as the Sun symbolizes a psychological faculty with six interrelated functions, so Uranus has its functions, too. Uranian activities are geared toward satisfying a set of interrelated needs symbolized by Aquarius. These include the need for awakening, liberation, progress, and perspective. As the active agent of these needs, Uranus signifies six complementary actions—objectifying, detaching, awakening, liberating, changing, and progressing. There is no single term that captures all these functions, though perhaps the *Observing Self* comes closest. In chapter 1, this was defined as the capacity to observe the contents of consciousness. Again, this capacity is linked to the six functions of Uranus:

1. **Objectifying**. The ability to stand outside and see something from an impersonal, detached **perspective**. To be objective is to be uninfluenced by subjective emotions or personal prejudices. An objective **overview** provides a broad, wholistic awareness, i.e., to perceive how the parts constitute the **whole** of a system, phenomenon, or situation.

2. **Nonattachment**, or **renunciation**. This is our capacity to *dis*identify with the contents of consciousness and give up attachment to things, people, and preferred experiences. It is the opposite of solar intentionality, or will. Nonattachment is related to the Buddhist concept of *impermanence*, which affirms that all phenomena are subject to continuous change.

3. **Awakening, enlightenment, revelation**. Capacity for spiritual and intellectual insight. To awaken is to shift one's perspective so that a broader and more humane understanding is liberated from the shackles of conventional thought. Enlightenment has a quality of revelation, i.e., manifestation of divine will or truth.

4. **Liberating, Emancipating**. To free something from oppression, confinement, or a stuck condition. Psychologically this can mean release from the strictures of false beliefs and negative, limited perspectives. Liberation makes possible the realization of human potential.

5. **Changing, Reforming, Innovating.** The ability to recognize and accept that nothing remains the same, and that reforms and innovations are necessary for the evolution of a system.

6. **Progress and Advancement.** The ability to develop and move forwards toward higher or better states. Progress means steady improvement, as well as the promotion of conditions, policies, or ideas that are of benefit to humanity. This may entail joining with others of like mind for a common cause.

Note that each of the above functions presupposes the others. The primary attribute of the Observing Self is to observe the contents of consciousness without judgment. **Objective witnessing** enables one to have experiences without identifying with them, i.e., without attachment or aversion. By disidentifying with both outer and inner contents, the individual is free to learn from new experiences. **Non-attachment** can lead to radical insight, awakening the individual to a broader, more comprehensive identity. New perspectives **liberate** the person from constricting beliefs that impoverish his experience. Emancipation from obsolete ideas and bankrupt policies naturally impels one toward **change,** reformist ideals, and innovative thinking. This, in turn, may lead to **advancement** of a cause that benefits humanity.

Now, let us take a closer look at the Observing Self and discover why it correlates to Uranus. In so doing, we will also explore that archetype that most closely corresponds to the functions of the Observing Self—the *Trickster*.

THE OBSERVING SELF

Because the Observing Self constitutes awareness of awareness, it transcends any specific content of consciousness. As such, it transcends any particular thought, feeling, or action, for it experiences these as objects. Deikman declares that the most important fact about the Observing Self is that it is incapable of being objectified. Whatever one can notice or conceptualize is an object of awareness, not awareness itself, which seems to step back when we experience an object. Unlike every other aspect of experience—thoughts, emotions, desires—the Observing Self can be known but not located, not "seen."[31]

As a psychological faculty, the Observing Self is a bridge between ordinary, self-consciousness and the transcendent realm of unitive consciousness. As such, it is our link to Universal Mind and the Cosmic Will. Philosopher Huston Smith points out that in all major religious traditions it is agreed that Universal Consciousness cannot be objectified or differentiated because it constitutes the very nature of all that is. Eastern philosophies depict it as an animated spirit that is infinitely diffused and therefore present as the very life in living things, e.g., Taoism regards it—Tao—as a spontaneous ordering principle in Nature. Such traditions depict Universal Mind as purposive, or intentional, in that all natural processes are evolving toward states of increasing unity. As a link to Cosmic Mind, the Observing Self broadens awareness and enables us to see how individual human beings are subsumed in a vast, evolutionary process.

To the extent that we identify with the Observing Self, we disidentify with our emotions and thoughts and remain receptive to the influx of a higher consciousness. While personal experience is temporal, the Observing Self is wired in to the infinite and the eternal. To identify with this higher ground means that self-esteem is no longer determined by the dominant experience of the moment. Like a still pond that reflects its surroundings without being changed by them, the Observing Self is unconditioned and radically open.

The capacity to observe experience without identifying with it is precisely what allows change to occur on lower, egoic levels. For example, we are not controlled by our negative beliefs to the extent that we can observe and question them. When we are able to take a reflective position in relation to our thoughts, feelings, and sensations, we are developing a state of equanimity. When we do not take this observing position, we become attached. We are immersed or captured by the contents of our interconnected mind moments.

Sigmund Freud, who had Sun conjunct Uranus, originated the method of free association, which is similar to Deikman's concept of the Observing Self. The word *free* refers to the patient's relative suspension of conscious control. Conscious control, of course, is the purview of the Sun, whereas its opposite—spontaneous freedom—is symbolized by Uranus. The point here is that one can choose to allow the contents of consciousness to freely flow without restriction or direction. Freud regarded free association as the methodological key to psychoanalysis. The patient is asked to express in words all thoughts, feelings, wishes, images, and memories, without reservation, as they spontaneously occur.

Freud knew from his own self-analysis that by giving up control and allowing an uncensored flow of information to suffuse consciousness one could be liberated from rigidified patterns of thought and feeling. The patient, however, must be receptive to contents that stream from a source other than his conscious mind, and to observe this content without judgment. As he expands his ability to free associate, i.e., to witness the stream of his own consciousness, he strengthens a balance between self-expression (Sun) and self-witnessing (Uranus). Free association thereby leads to progressive freedom from unconscious conflicts and conditioned response patterns.

Meditative techniques employ a similar strategy. For example, *vipassana* and *zazen* (different Buddhist meditation traditions) both emphasize continuous observation of mind content. Students are instructed simply to watch the stream of thoughts and impressions going through their minds without making judgments or attempting to control it. In both meditation and psychoanalysis, the goal is to extract the Observing Self from processes in which it tends to be submerged. As the aspirant distances herself from habitual thoughts and feelings, there is increased ability to experiment with new behaviors. Thus growth and change is a natural consequence of strengthening the Observing Self.

Note how different this is from solar processes of intentionality, creativity, and identification, all of which contribute to the development of a fixed identity and personal myth. Uranus is about shattering the myth and becoming aware of its arbitrary, constructed quality. Once the individual realizes that they are trapped in a story of their own authorship, this awareness can be liberating—like awakening from a trance. Rather than *being* the story, they realize they *have* a story and that the story can be changed.

The goal is to make the ego an object of awareness, not the purpose of one's life. The ego can be transcended or dissolved as the individual awakens to an identification with Universal Mind. Emotions, sensations, thoughts—these can be observed because they are temporal; they rise and fall, continually subject to change. The Uranian dimension, i.e., awareness *per se*, is knowable only by direct apprehension. We know it by realizing that we *are* the process of knowing. In higher meditative states, contents cease but awareness remains. This is knowing by identification, which is why we cannot observe it. We cannot detach ourselves from Universal Mind anymore than a wave can detach itself from the ocean.

In short, the Observing Self encompasses all six functions traditionally associated with Uranus: objective witnessing, non-attachment, revelation, liberation, change, and progress. While these functions have been discussed in terms that relate solely to the individual, in subsequent sections we will see how the Observing Self is also responsible for processes of change and discovery that advance the cause of the collective psyche.

The Trickster Archetype

As an archetype, several astrologers have connected Uranus to the mythic figure of Prometheus, and surely this is a valid identification.[32] However, if I were to choose one archetype that most closely corresponds to the Observing Self, I would choose the *Trickster*, also called the *Wise Fool, Court Jester,* or *Merry Prankster.*

As a metaphor for the unexpected, the Trickster is characterized by behaviors that are in opposition to egoic attitudes and conventional mind-sets. As such, it is the antithesis of the Ruler and the Hero archetypes. Characters who are primarily clowns or comical sidekicks express this archetype. According to Vogler, the trickster embodies energies of mischief and desire for change, and serves several important psychological functions:

> They cut big egos down to size, and bring heroes and audiences down to earth. By provoking healthy laughter they help us realize our common bonds, and they point out folly and hypocrisy. Above all, they bring about healthy change, often by drawing attention to the imbalance and absurdity of a stagnant psychological situation. They are the natural enemies of the status quo. When we are taking ourselves too seriously, the Trickster part of our personalities may pop up to bring back needed perspective.[33]

Likewise, the noted Jungian analyst, June Singer, asserts that the Trickster

> symbolizes that aspect of our nature that is ready to bring us down when we get inflated, or humanize us when we become pompous. He is the satirist par excellence, whose trenchant wit points out the flaws in our haughty ambitions, and makes us laugh though we may feel like crying. The major psychological function of the trickster figure is to make it possible for us to gain a sense of proportion about ourselves.[34]

Note the Uranian/Aquarian themes in the above descriptions—deflating big egos, comic relief, exposing hypocrisy, promoting change, and establishing perspective. The real life physician "Hunter Patch Adams", as depicted by Robin Williams in the 1997 movie *Patch Adams*, is a perfect example of the Trickster archetype. Adams dressed as a clown, wore a rubber nose and silly hat, shocked dying patients with bizarre tricks, used humor and laughter to heal, humanized medicine by collapsing the doctor-patient hierarchy, opened a free health clinic, and spearheaded a national movement to revolutionize the health care system. Like many other real life Trickster figures—among them Howard Stern, Jim Carrey, Woody Allen, Roseanne Barr, Steve Martin, and Bill Maher—Adams' Sun forms a close aspect to Uranus, in this case the conjunction.

A Link Between Human and Divine

In many myths, the Trickster is depicted as a not-quite-human being caught midway between the gods and mortals. The Trickster is alienated from humankind but also drawn irresistibly toward them. The half-god/half-human quality of the Trickster represents an integration of the Leo-Aquarius polarity.

In fact, Prometheus is a good example of the Trickster archetype, for as a Titan he begrudged the superiority of the Olympians and revenged himself by favoring mortals to the detriment of the gods. In an effort to help humankind, he tricked Zeus on a number of occasions, the most notable of which involved his theft of fire—a gift to the human race. Here, Prometheus models a Uranian revolt against the solar ego. Again, "the needs of the many {humanity} outweigh the needs of the few {gods}." As a demigod who identified with humans, Prometheus links the Aquarian and Leonine dimensions.

In Greek mythology, Prometheus' sacrificial act of stealing

fire—light—symbolizes the human capacity for enlightenment, and is analogous to the Christian myth of Jesus' sacrifice for the sins of Man, thereby making himself a link between human and divine. In effect, the true function of the Trickster is to awaken the individual to a broader, more cosmic perspective. Yet, there is a price to pay for this gift of fire. When Zeus punished Prometheus by chaining him to Mount Caucasus and sending an eagle to feed upon his liver during the day (which grew back again each night), Prometheus suffered willingly this apparent torture. According to Guirand, Prometheus was unrepentant and "persisted in his attitude of revolt."[35] Likewise, the human being must be willing to suffer humiliating defeat of the will in order to awaken a transegoic capacity for enlightened action.

TRICKSTERS AND THE MULTIPLICITY OF SELF

Recall that the function of the Sun is to create a unique, separate sense of self, a distinct identity of which we can be proud and that necessarily excludes less desirable ways of being. Conversely, the Trickster reminds us that personal identity is itself a myth, an arbitrary construction built upon an illusion of exclusivity. Pearson writes:

> The Fool is the element of the psyche that represents multiplicity of consciousness. Like the Court Fools who make fun of the King or Queen, the internal Fool (or Trickster) continually undercuts our sense of a unified self. It is responsible for Freudian slips and other indications that what the conscious mind thinks it wants is not the whole story. The Fool teaches us that we are always expressing our *selves* in the world, not a single self.[36]

The Fool naturally opposes the ego by revealing unrealized potentials and radical alternatives to one's current identity. Thus it reminds us to not take ourselves too seriously, for in the end one's current identity is but a story construction that must give way to ever new, more comprehensive versions.

The Trickster is so radically open that its identity is not even limited to a particular gender. "The most powerful Trickster figures are androgynous," writes Pearson, "and may express this through cross-dressing. They know what it is like to be both a man and a woman, and hence have a kind of wholeness that makes them not need a member of the opposite sex for a sense of completion."[37]

Radically open and unpredictable, the Fool finds a variety of outlets for the many facets of his personality, even if this puts him on the boundary of society. The Fool suffers a certain alienation from other people precisely because he is not identifiable with any one group or way of being, i.e., he cannot be *typed*. As Hillman reminds us, the psyche is far from being a unified singularity; rather, it is a polymorphous plurality that is only relatively integrated. The notion that one can *be* anything or anyone is joyfully expressed by that arch-Uranian, Maude, in the 1972 cult film *Harold and Maude*. At one point she breaks spontaneously into song:

> If you want to be free, be free,
> 'cause there's a million things to be,
> you know that there are.
> So if you want to be high, be high,
> If you want to be low, be low,
> 'cause there's a million ways to go,
> you know that there are.
> If you want to be me, be me,
> if you want to be you, be you,
> 'cause there's a million things to do,
> you know that there are.
> You can do what you want,

the opportunity's on,
and if you find a new way,
you can do it today.

A 79 year old free spirit, Maude exemplifies how Aquarius is embodied in the characteristics of old age. Recall from Chapter 1 that Aquarius represents the stage of 68-80 years, an eccentric time of life that is consistent with the psychology of the Fool. "In old age," claims Pearson, "the Fool teaches us to let go of the need for power and goals and achievement so that we can live each day as it comes."[38] To be eccentric means to be "off center, or off course," and this is precisely what the Fool personifies—a decentering of self that allows for the multiplicity of identities that are inherent in the psyche. The Wise Fool transcends the illusion of a unitary self and is able to express the diversity of his or her wholeness.

THE JESTER AND THE KING

The Trickster, as *Court Jester,* provided a natural counterpart to the Kings and Queens of medieval Europe. In the traditional court, the Jester was important because he provided a humanizing influence, i.e., he helped the King to not take himself too seriously. Fools can be immoral, anarchistic, and irreverent without fear of reprisal. "They have a license to say what other people would be hanged for," writes Pearson. Fools have permission "to puncture the Ruler's Ego when the Ruler is in danger of hubris, and to generally provide balance to the kingdom by breaking the rules and thereby allowing an outlet for forbidden insights, behaviors, and feelings."[39] By keeping things light and comical, the Fool could also provide a fresh perspective, thereby awakening the King to realities of which he was unawares.

Some good examples of the Fool our current culture is political satirist Jon Stewart of *The Daily Show,* whose Sun is in exact square to Uranus, and *Real Time's* Bill Maher who has Sun in Aquarius exactly opposed Uranus in Leo. Even the name of Maher's former TV show, *Politically Incorrect,* bears witness to his role as Court Jester who makes fun of the King (presidents). A classic example of the Fool was played by comic actor Danny Kaye in the delightful 1956 film, *The Court Jester,* which is considered one of the best comedies ever made, and possibly Kaye's finest performance. With his Sun conjunct Uranus within two degrees, Kaye was, as they say, "born for the part."

In his book, *The Fool and His Scepter,* Willeford asserts that the Jester and Ruler form a matched pair. As a symbol of the ego, the Ruler was always in danger of becoming rigid, attached to old ways, and obstructing necessary change. While the function of the King was to retain sovereignty, doing so necessarily negated alternative perspectives. Every choice, by definition, excluded its opposite, which is how kingdoms (and identities) are forged. Willeford states that the Jester provides an institutionalized link with the excluded forces and energies, and in so doing, embodies "the principle of wholeness, reinstating in measured form the primeval condition before the separation of the kingdom from that which it excludes."[40]

If the Ruler represents the Ego, which is built upon exclusion, then the Fool signifies a principle of wholeness. As such, says Pearson, the Fool supersedes the Ego and "represents the end of the [ego's] journey."[41] Of course, this is pure astrology, for Aquarius supersedes and completes the Leonine (heroic) journey. Fools teach us to keep changing, to embrace the new and the unexpected, even if this means suffering a defeat of our vaunted will. Only by establishing a link to Fool energy can we develop the resilience to overcome shock, flow with disruptions, and bounce back from disappointment. Like Wile E. Coyote, a classic Fool, we can step off cliffs, dash headlong into walls and get squashed by bulldozers, only to get up and try and try again.

The Fool reminds us, over and over, not to take ourselves too seriously. The ego's mistake is to see itself only as King—God's representative on earth—and never as Fool. In her classic work, *The Fool: His Social and Literary History,* Enid Welsford observes that comedy is serious literature because it is a foretaste of the truth: we are all more human than otherwise. Even the humanist must beware of self-inflation. "The Fool is wiser than the humanist," says Welsford, "and clownage is less frivolous than the deification of humanity."[42]

Ultimately, the Fool's purpose is to reveal alternative perspectives that allow us to see reality more whole. For this to occur, however, we must be tricked out of our usual behaviors, beliefs, and ways of perceiving. A Uranian mind-set is frequently hard to tell from madness, because it is so different from the ego's concern with appearances, propriety, and consensual reality. Indeed, one form of the Fool has always been the madman or madwoman. There are countless examples in myth, film, and literature, but a particularly good one is Lily Tomlin's character, Trudy, the bag lady.

In Tomlin's one-woman show, *The Search for Signs of Intelligent Life in the Universe,* Trudy tells how she experienced "the kind of madness Socrates talked about, a divine release of the soul from the yoke of custom and convention."[43] Trudy explains that "reality" is nothing more than a "collective hunch" and that, more so, it is "the leading cause of stress among those in touch with it." She decides to let it go. Thinking of the great jokes she plays now, she says, "I never could've done stuff like that when I was in my *right* mind. I'd be worried people would think I was crazy. When I think of the fun I missed I try not to be bitter."[44]

Pearson regards Trudy as a modern-day Wise Fool, whose loss of sanity opened her mind to the cosmos. She concludes that "the kind of enlightenment Trudy illustrates—the ability to celebrate one's life as a bag lady without needing money, status, a home, or even sanity—returns us to perfect freedom, and to innocence."[45]

THE FOOL AND THE HERO

Just as the Jester complements the Ruler, so the Fool is a natural counterpart to the Hero. Often depicted as the Hero's loyal and trusted sidekick, the Fool signifies qualities that are inconsistent with heroism. If the Hero is virtuous, strong, and good, the Fool may be disreputable, ineffectual, and mischievous. In *The Phantom Menace,* the bumbling and cowardly Jar-Jar Binks exemplifies the Trickster side-kick. He is opposite in every way to the Jedi heroes, Qui-Gon and Obi-Wan Kenobi.

The partnership of the Fool and the Hero signifies that in order to become whole the ego-self needs to make an ally of precisely those traits that are *its* opposite. In doing so, a quality emerges that expands the boundaries of the self. This is symbolized in myth by the solution to a dilemma that emerges out of the dialogue between Hero and sidekick. In *Phantom,* it was Jar-Jar Binks who forged an alliance between the Jedi and the Gungan, a race of amphibious creatures that proved indispensable in defeating the evil invaders.

Here we see how a partnership between the Solar and Uranian dimensions of the psyche is empowering, for it yields a certain balanced outlook that neither side possesses of itself. The Hero provides a strong will and raw courage, but the Fool provides an objective perspective. Jar-Jar knew the lay of the land, so to speak, and had group connections that were necessary for the Jedi's heroic conquest.

Remember, the solar part of us has an attachment to a desired outcome—to triumph and victory. Uranus, however, signifies the fertile chaos of the unexpected. It is only when our egos have developed a proper relationship to the internal Fool-sidekick, that we can "trust the process" and allow life to unfold organically. Otherwise, our hubris-ridden egos will unduly intervene, assuming rights and forcing outcomes that lead invariably to humiliation.

Chapter Three

Noble King, Wise Fool

ASPECTS BETWEEN THE SUN AND URANUS

Anytime the Sun forms an aspect to Uranus, the Leo-Aquarius polarity is going to be highlighted. Accordingly, a dominant theme in the life of the native will be the challenge of integrating these two signs and their planetary representatives. Whereas the sextile and trine suggest a relatively easy time of it, every other aspect, including and especially the quincunx, signifies a challenge.

How can one have both an individual and a collective identity? *That* is the dilemma to be faced. Uranus is a reminder of one's ordinariness, i.e., that one is merely human, one of billions. Conversely, the Sun struggles to express that one is, in fact, a special person. How can the individual express both truths concurrently? Hard aspects suggest a potential conflict between attachment and non-attachment, pride and humility, egotism and altruism. As these aspects are integrated over time, the individual may come to embody a commitment to conscious evolution, recognition of impermanence, and emancipation from the dictates of pride. However, if hard aspects are not integrated, the individual may evidence egocentric radicalism, instability of identity, and/or fear of change.

If one planet is expressed at the expense of the other, this leads to an unbalanced state as evidenced, for example, by either a narcissistic (Solar) or schizoid (Uranian) disorder. Accordingly, the first half of this chapter focuses on thematic variations of a lack of integration, as expressed in childhood experiences and subsequent personality organizations.

Conversely, in the second half, we will focus on exemplars of an integrated Sun-Uranus as expressed through personality attributes, creative works, scientific accomplishments, and heroic humanitarianism. To show how these aspects can be actualized at a higher level, I place special emphasis on Uranus as the Trickster archetype and explain why liberation of awareness from the tyranny of the ego is an antidote to the hubris that is inherent in the Sun.

LACK OF INTEGRATION

To the extent that Sun-Uranus aspects are not integrated, the individual will tend to express one side while suppressing the other. This does not necessarily manifest as an obvious "either-or" expression, e.g., the person is either arrogant *or* altruistic, but has elements of each, such as arrogant altruism. The problem is that one side is expressed consciously and the other unconsciously. Generally, the conscious side will be excessive, while the unconscious, shadow component will operate in a problematic, subversive manner, thus undermining the person's conscious intentions. Each function—Sun *and* Uranus—will tend to become bloated and extreme in an effort to ward off the pressure of the other. In short, there is reciprocal influence with mutual resistance.

With the Sun in hard aspect to Uranus, often the person will feel alienated from conventional society, being odd, eccentric, or different in some way. Despite or perhaps because of their outsider identity, there is a strong need to rebel against the status quo—whether at home, work, or society in general.

While they may feel ahead of their time, with a breadth of vision and progressive ideals that place them at odds with traditional viewpoints, more often their apparent altruism is contaminated by unmet egoic needs for validation and approval. Accordingly, the individual may be prone to fanaticism, bigotry, and intolerance of those who oppose their hubris-saturated vision of a better world.

Behavior can vacillate between an arrogant radicalism on the one hand, and a deflated, negativistic attitude on the other. This latter condition is characterized by a self-perception of being disliked for being different, which may turn into self-contempt, "I'm different and that's bad." Or, the individual might experience him- or herself as having no importance, value, or significance in the grand scheme of things. This state is characterized by a loss of confidence, paralyzing self-doubt, and painful uncertainty about one's true purpose in life.

SOME ANIMALS ARE MORE EQUAL THAN OTHERS

If the Sun preempts Uranus without reducing its egoic grandiosity, then the individual will display pretensions of superiority within the Uranian realm, which is at best a contradiction. One is the "greatest" revolutionary against the elite, a "superior" radical that denounces aristocracy, or the "most enlightened" of the enlightened. It's like the famous line in George Orwell's *Animal Farm,* "All animals are equal, but some animals are more equal than others."

This kind of egoism is quite apparent in Dennis Rodman (Sun-Uranus square), the formerly outrageous "bad-boy" of professional basketball with his ever-changing fluorescent hair and body-covering tattoos. A flagrant non-conformist, Rodman cross-dresses in public, flaunted his defiance of the NBA, and posed nude on a motorcycle for the cover of his first book, *Bad as I Wanna Be.* Anicka Rodman, his ex-wife who countered with her own book, *Worse Than He Says He Is,* writes that Dennis either expresses himself "in a court jester sort of way" with his hair color and woman's clothes, or he uses violence. In other words, we have an unintegrated Sun-Uranus square. Either Rodman makes a spectacle (Sun) out of his Uranian impulses, or, failing to control the outcome, he reacts violently, as when he head-butted a referee in a 1996 game against the New Jersey Nets.

While defending his image as a bad-boy iconoclast, "I'm just an individual," one can't help but notice the desperate need for approval that underlies his outlandish behavior. As Patricia Holt writes, "If he weren't so obviously frightened and overcompensating, perhaps all his posturing would be amusing."[46] Rodman exemplifies how a tricksterian impulse to shock can be perverted into self-aggrandizing exhibitionism. Fancying himself a rock star of mega-proportions, he once claimed: "You can put me up there with Jim Morrison, Jimi Hendrix and Janis Joplin. They say Elvis is dead. I say, no, you're looking at him. Elvis isn't dead, he just changed color."[47] But Rodman's antics give the impression that he hasn't truly chosen his anti-hero stance; rather, he is possessed by it. His compulsion to be "different" masquerades as individualism, but like the female attire he publicly flaunts, his performance is more pretend than real.

In fact, Uranus is not about being an individual, which is precisely the problem when it aspects the Sun. Uranus is about evolving beyond individuality toward a collective identity. Whereas the Sun wants validation for being special, Uranus is pulled in the opposite direction—toward humility and self-effacement. This internal conflict can be foreshadowed by experience with important figures in childhood, especially with a father who devalues or belittles his child, the consequence of which is that the child does not develop a clear, differentiated sense of self.

Archetypally it would seem that this type of experience is in the service of developing a sense of self-proportion, as if the Universe is requiring the individual to become less egocentric and more altruistic. However, if the Uranian imperative is overwhelming to the nascent ego, it can backfire and result in a developmental fixation around the unmet solar need. This may express itself later as a narcissist who desperately needs to be seen as special—yet, is compelled to rebel against this need by behaving in an outlandish, anti-conformist manner. Such conflicted behavior is, in effect, an unconscious quest for attention even while assuring that the attention received is of a negative variety.

The Sun-Uranian Father and Its Consequences

The Solar meaning of father is different from its Saturnian counterpart. As Saturn, the father represents authority and teaches the child discipline, responsibility, and how to succeed in the outer world. As Sun, the father is the child's first and best playmate, chief admirer, and devoted fan. In other words, the father's solar function is to validate the child and help him/her develop self-esteem.

When Uranus forms a hard aspect to the Sun, however, the father might be distant and detached, erratic in his attention, inconsistent, or in some other way not a stable, reliable figure. If the father plays negative Trickster, he can deflate, humiliate, and undercut the child's developing identity. The result is that the child does not receive the attention or validation he needs to develop trust in his capacity to make good choices.

An unstable relationship to father can result in a deflated, unstable sense of self. Lack of attention leads to feelings of insignificance and low self-esteem, which may later result in a compensatory grandiosity. This, apparently, was the case with Rodman, whose father suddenly stopped coming home when Rodman was three. In his biography, Rodman describes how for months afterwards he wandered around the house in a daze, wondering what he did to make his father go away. He never saw or heard from his father again.[48]

Sometimes, too, the father can be so deflated that he overcompensates and tries to monopolize all the solar energy for himself. He demands to be treated as the conquering hero, whether he deserves it or not. Conversely, the child is required to carry negative Trickster energy and may do so with a vengeance, embodying all those characteristics that are inconsistent with heroism. Underneath, however, the youngster is being made to feel unimportant relative to the father (or mother if Sun is in the 4th).

If the child wins a contest or gets good grades, the father may react as if somehow this diminishes *his* importance. He may then ignore the child, devalue the child's accomplishment, scold the child for getting "a big head," or berate the child for not doing better. The underlying message is "I'm still top dog around here, so don't even think about competing with *Me*." All of this represents a splitting of the Solar-Uranus aspect, with the parent keeping the good half, and projecting onto the child the bad. Unable to be the Hero, the child is forced to play the negative Fool—unimportant, insignificant, and ineffectual.

Children with this sort of father may develop the idea that positive attention results in punishment and thus is to be avoided. In adulthood, this can be acted out in a number of ways: (1) sabotaging one's intentions through a pattern of unreliable, inconsistent behavior—e.g., quitting or "cutting out" in the middle of a competition; or (2) developing a defiant, devil-may-care attitude toward those who are in a position to evaluate one's performance.

In other words, the individual beats fate to the punch by purposefully behaving in a non-conforming way that is likely to cause rejection. Then s/he can say, "See, I don't need approval; I choose to be different. If people can't accept that, it's their problem." In so doing, the Sun-Uranus person gains the advantage by appearing to control the very thing he fears—belittlement. Rather than trying to gain positive attention, the individual displays a *reaction formation*, i.e., he does the opposite. If the desire for approval and validation causes anxiety, then the person reacts by appearing to not need approval. An anti-solar reaction formation, however, may be marked by extravagant showiness—the person protests too much—and by compulsiveness, "I *must* not need approval." Extreme forms of behavior of any kind usually denote a reaction formation.

Clearly this is evident in Rodman's compulsive non-conformity and exaggerated displays of rebelliousness. Uranus, in other words, is overfunctioning in reaction to his solar needs, which are operating unconsciously because they pose a threat. That he has become possessed by his solar needs—for attention, notoriety, and fame—may not occur to him. Cook writes, "He is everywhere, emptily. He is in your face in movies, TV, bookstores, video games, action figures and virtual reality, but he says you don't really know him."[49] Yet, Rodman himself brags that he is the equivalent of a Hendrix, Joplin, or Elvis. "Elvis isn't dead, he just changed color."

Rodman's identification with these larger than life, mythical figures illustrates what can happen when the Sun/son does not receive sufficient attention from a solar (father) figure. Unable to develop a clear, individual identity, the person becomes absorbed into the collective (Uranian) sphere and appropriates a mythic figure with which to identify. The ego, in other words, has not integrated the Uranian dimension; rather, it has become possessed by it. All the cravings of the ego remain intact, but are now transferred to a dimension of consciousness that symbolizes wholeness and completion. Thus, the person feels himself to be the all-important One who transcends ordinary humanity. As Rodman put it, "Once I learned to be myself, the rest just happened. And now I'm in the atmosphere. I am the reality. I'm Elvis, Jimi Hendrix and the Grateful Dead all wrapped into one. The president of the United States gets a hard-on just thinking about me."[50]

Someone with Sun-Uranus pathology may also have an identity that is continually shifting. If, in fact, there is no stable self-image, then choosing to be someone who is constantly changing is a defense against the pain of not knowing who one is. Rodman, for example, writes that he didn't know who he was until he was 32, though it is debatable even now whether he has a clear, well integrated sense of self. "I am a multicolored individual. A different color every day...I'm the fucking chameleon," says Rodman.

After contemplating suicide when he was 31, Rodman describes in his autobiography how he decided instead to kill the conformist in himself. "At ten paces I turned and shot the imposter. I killed the Dennis Rodman that had tried to conform to what everybody wanted him to be."[51] In other words, Uranus shot—reacted against—the Sun. The goal was to free himself of any need for approval. Yet, his wild and crazy guy antics—cross dressing, makeup, tattoos, outlandish clothes, and different hair color for every game—may simply be a substitute for an authentic sense of self. It is also a desperate, albeit unconscious, ploy for attention.

The Case of Trickster Howard Stern

Analysis of the Trickster archetype would not be complete without at least a brief commentary on the irrepressible Howard Stern. Stern, whose Sun opposes Uranus, is the outrageous and irreverent bad-boy of talk radio. The original "shock jock", Stern gained fame for interviews with celebrities during which he would discuss every sort of bodily function, perversion, and sexual act that crossed his mind. He has been fined hundreds of thousands of dollars for indecency by the FCC, which only seems to increase his popularity. His 1993 autobiography, *Private Parts*, was the fastest selling autobiography of all time and was subsequently made into a movie.

After a mediocre start as a radio disc jockey, Stern discovered the talent that would put him over the top: saying on air absolutely anything that came into his head. This was Stern's version of free association—uncensored, unedited, spontaneous discharge of all mental contents, especially those that had to do with forbidden subjects like sex and hostility. The more outrageous and uncensored he became, the more attention and notoriety he received.

In this regard, Stern is much like Rodman. Both discovered that by living an uncensored life they could liberate themselves from any need for approval. It was also their ticket to fame. Whereas Rodman decided to "kill" the conformist in himself, Stern writes of his decision: "To kill my competition…I was going to say whatever the fuck I wanted to say."[52]

Like Rodman, Stern posed for the cover of his first book, *Private Parts*, in the nude. And for the cover of his second book, *Miss America*, he dressed in drag—again like Rodman. Recall Pearson's comment that the Trickster symbolizes the multiplicity of consciousness and often manifests as an androgynous being capable of shifting between male and female forms.

Stern is not only completely uncensored in the comments he makes to and about others, he is equally candid about himself. In *Private Parts* he describes his tortured adolescence, his penis inferiority complex, and his sexual proclivities in shocking (of course) detail. While he can be cruel, Stern generally reserves his cruelty for people whose fame and hubris make them open targets. In true Trickster fashion, he dismantles the whole notion of celebrity and deflates those who may be overly attached to their star status.

His childhood, predictably, was not pleasant or stable. When describing his narcissistic father, Stern actually refers to him as "King Ben". "King Ben would come home and sit on his throne and everything had to be just right," writes Stern.[53] The problem was that rather than making the King laugh, Stern merely succeeded in making him angry. In response to his father's compensatory King status, Howard had to play the negative Fool so as not to compete with him. No matter what Howard said or did, his father would scream at him, tell him to shut up, and call him names like "idiot," "moron," "dummy," and "dope." Stern confesses, "Being called a moron to me was real. I thought I *was* a moron."[54]

As mentioned, humiliation at the hands of the father is a common experience with an unintegrated Sun-Uranus aspect. The elder Stern exemplifies how a Sun-Uranus father is frequently too narcissistic to support his child's self-esteem or individuation. When Howard was still a young boy, he told his father that he wanted to be a millionaire. His father responded by flying into a rage and chasing him up on the stairs, "He wanted to beat the shit out of me," Howard recalls, presumably in retaliation for Howard's implicit ambition to be more successful than him.

Stern's father complained that he was the *only* one who could do anything right; yet, he would neither allow nor encourage Howard to succeed. If Howard attempted to mow the lawn, for example, "King Ben" would scream at him and take over the job. In fact, the elder Stern continually shrieked at Howard that he was too lazy, stupid, or incompetent to succeed at anything. After Howard graduated from college with honors, his father sneered disparagingly, "So what are you going to do now, idiot?" Howard reminded his father that he had graduated magna cum laude. "Shut up!" his father screamed. "I paid twenty grand for that degree. I never went to college!"[55]

One suspects that the humiliation Stern experienced at the hands of his father now fuels the outrageousness that characterizes his career as a talk show host. At last, he can say anything he wants. If the FCC or his boss tell him to "shut up!" Howard merely becomes more offensive. Ever the Trickster, his compulsion to rebel against, and to shock and deflate, those who "take themselves too seriously" is transparent for all to see—and hear.

IDENTITY DISORDER

If the Sun is about making a commitment, i.e., a clear choice, and Uranus is about remaining open to the unexpected, then a square between these two principles can be experienced as difficulty making commitments. The underlying fear is that it's all going to change anyway, so why bother? If the world is not stable or consistent, then neither can be the self; thus the person is prone to erratic, self-defeating behavior. As soon as the Sun makes a decision, Uranus wants to change course entirely—again, beat fate to the punch. The end result is that the person feels scattered and uncertain. Again, Rodman is a prime example, for he was notorious for his unpredictability and unreliability as a team player.

Not surprisingly, the pathology of Sun-Uranus has to do with lack of identity. The ego's needs may be so unconscious that there is no center—no *me*—from which the individual can relate to the world. This is reflected in a condition known as Identity Disorder, which is described at length in the *Diagnostic and Statistical Manual of Mental Disorders (DSM IV)*.* The essential feature of Identity Disorder is an inability to reconcile aspects of the personality into a relatively coherent and acceptable sense of self. Such individuals are uncertain about a variety of issues relating to self-image, including

---

* DSM IV is the standard diagnostic text published by the American Psychiatric Association. For more information on how signs/planets correlate to specific personality disorders, see "Psychopathology of the Zodiac," in Mapping the Landscape of the Soul, Chapter 3, by G. Perry (2012c).

long term goals, career choice, friendship patterns, religious identification, moral values, sexual orientation, and group loyalties. Self-alienation is mirrored by the alienation one feels from society.

In effect, there is a disorder of will; the individual cannot *decide* what to do, what he believes, who he likes, and so forth. Behavior is unpredictable, with difficulty either in making choices or erratic experimentation. As Rodman put it, "My things are never planned...my life is a circus, 365 days of fucking confusion....I keep Lucifer wondering, What will he do next?"[56]

Negative or oppositional patterns are often chosen in an attempt to establish an independent identity distinct from other individuals. Such attempts may be manifested as transient experimental phases of widely divergent behavior as the individual "tries on" various roles. When Rodman was asked if he ever tries on women's clothing in private, he replied "I wear it once in a while. It shows that I am not just an athlete. It shows that I'm not afraid of society. I'm unconventional."[57] Yet, with identity disorder, mild anxiety is common and the native is plagued with self-doubt. Frequently, the disturbance is epitomized by the individual asking the question, "Who am I?"

THE SCHIZOID PERSONALITY

Perhaps the most disturbing and extreme manifestation of an unintegrated Sun-Uranus is *schizoid disorder*. The term schizoid is from the Greek, schizo – "to split." Psychologically speaking, this refers to the tendency to split off (dissociate from) psychological contents that are too difficult to bear. In other words, there is a splitting off from body, feelings, and ego so that just a disembodied mind remains. Part of the personality is detached and observing the rest of the self.

Note the similarity in this description with the Observing Self. In fact, the Observing Self is involved, but with schizoid disorder the psyche has more or less collapsed *into* the Observing Self so that everything else—feelings, urges, sensations—are comparatively asleep. This would be like having all of one's psychic energy funneled into Uranus so that nothing is left to activate the functions of the other planets. Conversely, individuals that have attained an integration with the Observing self have a capacity to objectify psychic contents yet without losing the ability to simultaneously experience these contents—e.g., feelings remain strong and vivid, sensations are sharp, intentions are clear, and there is a warmth and aliveness to the personality. In short, Uranus is active, but not to the exclusion of the other planets.

The criteria in DSM IV describes the schizoid disordered person as having a flat, cold demeanor, little interest in sexuality, and indifferent to others reactions to them. Like a stereotypical computer nerd, schizoids are loners without any apparent yearning for relationship. In fact, there is a defect in the capacity to form attachments. This is the "social misfit," the loner, oddball, or "weirdo" who marches to the beat of a different drummer. Such individuals generally appear remote and aloof, preferring to pursue solitary interests and hobbies rather than involve themselves with other people. There is an absence of warmth or interest in the feelings of others, and they may appear equally indifferent to praise or criticism. Often they seem absentminded and detached from their environment, as if "in a fog".

Individuals with this disorder are usually unable to express hostility. Similar to Identity Disorder, they may seem vague about their goals and indecisive in their actions. Because of a lack of social skills, they frequently never date or marry. Again, the core of the problem is actually a lack of ego or, more accurately, a denial of ego; the individual has no need to express or seek validation of an identity that is not consciously felt. Isolated and self-sufficient, they seem to be saying, "I need nothing and no one."

Intellectualization is a primary defense, which correlates to Uranus/Aquarius being an air/mental function. Yet, by cutting off from feelings and people, schizoids also cut themselves off from their capacity to love—i.e., from their solar function. Recall that a primary attribute of Leo and the Sun is romance. In a more general sense, this means to validate, court, and appreciate others. Yet, this is precisely what the schizoid cannot express and, more importantly, cannot receive.

If there was one game that most typified this personality style, it would be "hide and seek." On the one hand, the schizoid experiences others as hiding from them; thus they feel lonely and cut off from human contact. At other times, they are hiding from everyone else, as if the person fears being "seen" and "known". Schizoids seem to equate attention with being found out, intruded upon, and violated. Whether hiding or seeking, the individual is unable to establish meaningful attachments.

In fact, the real difficulty with schizoid disorder has to do with attachment. The consensus opinion is that the etiology of schizoid disorder lies in a failure to establish a secure attachment with a parental figure during childhood, e.g., there might have been some rupture or trauma in an important early relationship. Subsequently, the schizoid person has difficulty forming adult attachments, either avoiding them or forming insecure, clinging attachments. Attachment in this sense can be defined in a Taurean context, meaning a stable, secure relationship with a loving other. Unable to trust in this, the schizoid lives in terror of important people deserting them. I suspect, however, that schizoid disorder also is a consequence of another kind of failed attachment.

In *Part I*, I discussed how solar attachment is necessary in the formation of identity. By "solar attachment' I mean we get attached to beliefs, people, and values—whatever it is that we have *chosen*—for by our choices we create an identity and we want this identity to be positive. In particular, we become attached to the fulfillment of our intentions. But this requires validation from an outside source. We want our will to prevail and to be rewarded with approval—the "Yes!" experience that accompanies triumph of the will.

Aquarius, on the other hand, has to do with detachment, or non-attachment, which can be defined as a willingness for things to not work out the way one intends. The problem, however, is that if there is too much change, so that one experiences a more or less chronic frustration of the will, then intentionality itself can be abdicated. One simply stops trying; or, if one does try, it is accompanied by an anxious, uncertain commitment, as if one expects defeat. This negative expectation underlies the schizoid's conviction that "something is wrong with me," and is the basis of an inner emptiness, despair, and self-contempt.

I submit that schizoid disorder is a Sun-Uranus condition that results from a more or less chronic frustration of the will. For the condition is characterized by an excess of Uranian attributes—e.g., detachment, lack of emotionality, distancing, aloofness, flatness of affect, over-intellectuality, paralysis of will, indifference to others, romantic disinterest, social isolation—and a deficiency of solar attributes, e.g., lack of clear, sustained intentions. We can speculate, therefore, that hard aspects between the Sun and Uranus, including the conjunction, may result in a schizoid disorder in extreme cases.*

---

* Of course, there are a variety of ways that this can show up in a chart, including oppositions between planets in Leo and planets in Aquarius, Sun in the 11th house, Uranus in the 5th, oppositions between 5th house and 11th house planets, and various other combinations. Also, one never knows the degree to which these factors have been integrated, so it would be irresponsible and inaccurate to assert that schizoid disorder is always a consequence of these factors.

Unabomber Ted Kaczynski

One such extreme case that has received a great deal of public attention is that of Ted Kaczynski, the infamous Unabomber. From 1978 to 1996, Kaczynski waged a one-man terrorist campaign against the 'techno-industrial system of modern society'. He killed three people and maimed 23 others with elaborate homemade bombs that he sent via the postal system to specific targeted individuals at universities, airlines, biotechnology companies, and advertising agencies.

Kaczynski's enveloping madness is detailed in a 47-page psychiatric study that was prepared by Sally Johnson, M.D., a renowned federal prison psychiatrist who interviewed Kaczynski for more than 19 hours. She also interviewed his family and reviewed his copious writings on the bombings. Her report confirms that Kaczynski, who has a conjunction between his Sun and Uranus within one degree of arc (as well as a square from Uranus to the Moon), is a classic case of schizoid personality disorder with paranoid features.*

Kaczynski was the oldest son of a house wife and sausage maker. He told Johnson that he suffered "extreme verbal and emotional abuse" from his parents, though subsequent interviews with family members failed to corroborate his claims. His brilliance enabled him to skip the 6th grade, which he recalls as a pivotal event in his life. "He remembers not fitting in with the older children and being the subject of considerable verbal abuse and teasing from them," the report said.[58] It may be, however, that young Theodore Kaczynski simply lacked the parental support and/or the

---

* No doubt there are other ways that Uranus and Aquarius can show up in the chart of a schizoid prone individual. Also schizoid disorder is not a discrete entity. It occurs on a continuum from a mild feature to a severe personality disorder. Just as Uranus exists in every chart, most of us have a little schizoid in ourselves. All of these considerations, therefore, needed to be taken into account in diagnosing an individual, or in designing a research project to test astrological correlations to schizoid traits.

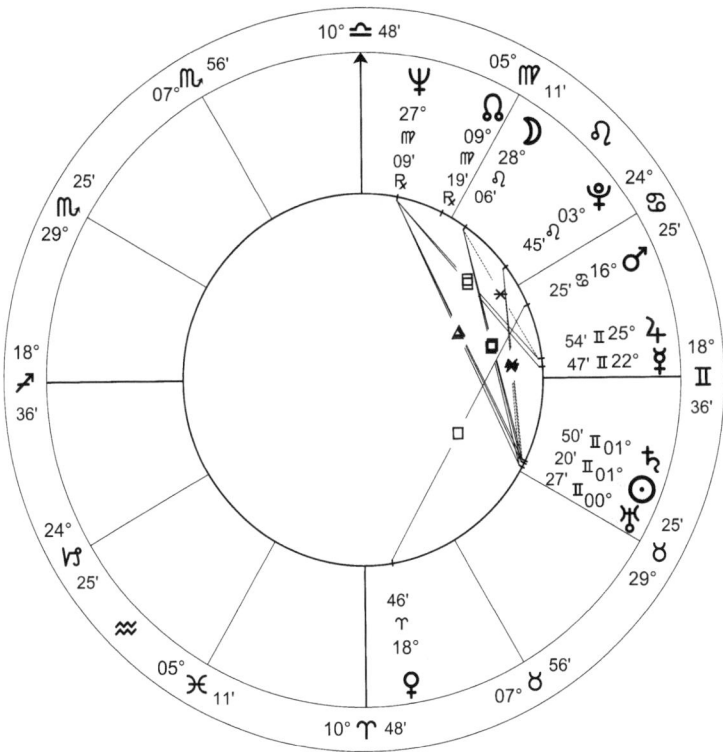

Figure 1: Ted Kaczynski. May 22, 1942, 8:30pm, Chicago, IL

ego-strength to stand up to the testing and teasing that is an inescapable part of a boy's life.

Kaczynski was described by his mother as a precocious child who "sometimes slipped in and out of his own world. There were times when he would retreat to his attic room and not want to be disturbed. Other times, he seemed to be in a trance, as if a veil would descend and he would shut others out as if in a catatonic state."[59] With a genius IQ of 170, Kaczynski graduated from high school at 16 and was awarded a scholarship to Harvard. Yet, his fear of rejection and lack of social skills precluded him from making friends. Note the Uranian-Schizoid themes already in evidence—social isolation, emotional withdrawal, and detachment.

While attending Harvard, Kaczynski grew increasingly isolated and unhappy. Frustrated with his inability to form relationships, he actually considered getting a sex change operation. Kaczynski would become sexually excited when he fantasized himself as a woman, yet because he was *not* a woman he was unable to obtain any sexual relief. Here again, we see shades of the gender/identity confusion that is characteristic of an unintegrated Sun-Uranus aspect.

By the 1990's, Kaczynski was blaming his parents for turning him into a social misfit. He accused them of being cruel and insensitive, and of being the reason for his reclusive nature. In a 1991 letter to his brother, Kaczynski tried in dramatic fashion to cut himself off from his family completely. "Cutting off" and severing ties is, again, typical of an unintegrated Sun-Uranus aspect. "I have got to know, I have GOT TO, GOT TO, GOT TO know," Kaczynski wrote, "that every last tie joining me to this stinking family has been cut FOREVER and that I will NEVER have to communicate with any of you again."[60]

While no parent is perfect, I suspect that he was looking for a scapegoat to blame for his own debilitating self-contempt. According to Dr. Johnson's psychiatric report, "Mr. Kaczynski is extremely sensitive to even minor criticism and tends to perceive this, or even an absence of encouragement or positive response from an individual, as a deliberate attempt at humiliation or harassment."[61]

When Uranus conjoins the Sun, the sense of self can be so fragile that there is not sufficient confidence and self-esteem to express one's will—i.e., to compete. Given that Uranus rules the collective psyche, it is extremely interesting that Kaczynski reports that he had dreams in which, "I would feel that organized society was hounding me with accusation in some way, or that organized society was trying in some way to capture my mind."[62]

From an astrological perspective, one has the impression that the collective dimension of the psyche—Uranus—has impinged upon the personal dimension—the Sun—and rendered it dysfunctional. In a healthy individual, a contact between the Sun and Uranus helps the person develop humility and a sense of self-proportion. However, if Uranus shocks the Sun too much, humility becomes humiliation, and self-proportion collapses into self-negation.

Recall Rodman's claim that he sought to kill the part of him that needed approval from others. Kaczynski, too, hated the part of himself (Sun) that needed love and validation. As is frequently the case, however, he transformed his self-hatred into a hatred of others. Dr. Johnson wrote "He frequently expressed both hatred and a wish for revenge and a love and affection for the same individual." Ultimately, Kaczynski converted his self-contempt into a desire to kill society at large, i.e., the collective psyche.

When Kaczynski imagined that he was perceived as a freak by other people, he would become enraged; yet, he could not express his anger openly (a common schizoid trait). Instead, he distanced himself and indulged in frequent fantasies of revolt and revenge. It wasn't until he quit his job as a math professor at UC-Berkeley in 1967, however, that his hatred of society took a lethal turn. Kaczynski retreated to a remote wilderness area in Montana where he built a tiny, one room shack with no electricity or running water. There, he began constructing his bombs and plotting his revenge.

We know that Uranus is associated with experiences that are shocking. It is significant, therefore, that the symptoms of schizoid disorder are similar to those of shock. For example, a person that has gone into shock after a traumatic incident seems to be dissociated from his surroundings. He appears pale because his blood has retreated from the surface of his skin and contracted inwards, as if in retreat from the outer threat. This is why shock victims get cold and start to shiver. We know, of course, that this is the body's way of protecting itself from anticipated harm, for if the blood retreats from the surface of the skin there is less bleeding and thus greater capacity to sustain life if one is cut or punctured.

The point is, with schizoid disorder, the person appears as if they are in a state of chronic shock. One dissociates from inner and outer experience to such an extent that the person feels and looks like a walking corpse; affect goes flat, feelings are numb, and the personality is bland and colorless. The individual appears to be an automaton with all the blood drained from the soul.

We can deduce, therefore, that the schizoid disordered person is afraid of something, and might have suffered a shock at a critical juncture in their development. Schizoid defenses are designed to ward off a reoccurrence of the traumatic event. In the summer of 1991, Kaczynski wrote to his mother that his early life had been shaped by traumatic social experiences that had left him profoundly wary of others. The following excerpt is particularly interesting in light of Kaczynski's allusion to "shock" as a metaphor for what happened to him.

> Suppose that for a period of years whenever you touched — let us say — a banana, you got a severe electric shock. After that you would always be nervous around bananas, even if you knew they weren't wired to shock you. Well, in the same way, the many rejections, humiliations and other painful influence (sic) that I underwent during adolescence at home, in high school, and at Harvard have conditioned me to be afraid of people. This fear or rejection based on bitter experience both at home and at school has ruined my life, except for the few years that I spent alone in the woods, largely out of contact with people.[63]

Kaczynski's letter demonstrates how the schizoid is afraid that others will impinge on him in ways that are shocking and upsetting. His withdrawal and isolation from society can be understood as a defense against this impingement. Again, from an astrological standpoint, Uranus tends to shatter the boundaries of the Sun so that the sense of having an individual self is compromised by an influx of collective energies. If one can handle such contents, and ground them to constructive benefit, then there is an ability to express oneself in a manner that contributes to the greater good of the greater whole. Like Freud, Newton, Descartes, and other geniuses of the Sun-Uranus variety, there can be discoveries that enlighten and liberate the masses.

Kaczynski was a genius, too, but he could not contain the powerful Uranian forces that engulfed him. Without sufficient ego boundaries to protect himself from the slings and arrows of life's misfortunes, he was simply too vulnerable. As Dr. Johnson confirmed, Kaczynski was so sensitive to even minor criticism that he perceived it as a deliberate attempt to humiliate or harass him.

Uranus, we know, has to do with the collective self, or society at large. To the extent that one has integrated the Uranus/Aquarian dimension, there is a sense of self-proportion, and a recognition of the importance of humanity over and above the self. Thus, Uranus/Aquarius is concerned with civil rights, humanitarian aid, and causes that benefit the whole. If, however, one has not sufficiently developed a clear, bounded sense of self, then Uranian energies can be experienced as overpowering and uncontrollable.

In various letters to his family, Kaczynski described how he feared socialization. From his perspective, society had the terrible power to socialize, which meant to take over his mind, to subsume him. Of course, society—the collective psyche—is not really some monstrous entity that has the power to possess a person and annihilate his individual self-hood. If, however, one does not have a strong sense of self, then the power of society can be perceived in just such a monstrous light.

Kaczynski wrote that he felt violated and brainwashed by society to such an extent that he was incapable of overcoming his inhibitions to fight back.

> My training has been quite successful in this regard. And the strength of my inhibitions is such that I don't believe I could ever commit a serious crime. Knowing my attitude toward psychological manipulation of the individual by society, you can imagine how humiliating it is for me to admit to myself that I have been successfully manipulated.[64]

Of course, eventually Kaczynski did overcome his inhibitions. Once Uranus appropriates the Sun for its own purposes, the individual is caught up in a whirlpool of psychic energy that consumes him. Ultimately, Kaczynski's life was reduced to a 20 year-long rebellion against society. Cut off from his solar nature, he lost his capacity for self-love and, by extension, his capacity to love others. Accordingly, when he chose his victims it was not personal. They were not real people to Kaczynski, just symbols of the techno-industrial state that he perceived as impinging.

Kaczynski described how when he read the paper, he became consumed with fury. "I would build up too much tense and frustrated anger against politicians, dictators, businessmen, scientists, communists, and others in the world who were doing things that endangered me or changed the world in ways I resented."[65] In the early 1970's, Kaczynski wrote the infamous manifesto that summarized his belief that scientific and technological progress would cause the extinction of individual liberty.

Note here, the classic Uranian themes of change, progress, and technology. Yet, Kaczynski was opposed to these things. Why? Because from the perspective of his Sun, they were engulfing him.* It was as if Uranus' conjunction of his Sun and square to his Moon threatened to eclipse his very self. This internal state of siege, however, was externalized into a conviction that society was threatening his individual liberty.

Kaczynski admitted that his discovery of a road newly cut through a Montana wilderness near his cabin was the precipitating event that turned him into a one-man revolution. On a walk in the woods one day, Kaczynski discovered the new road in a wild sanctuary that had been his refuge. "From that point on," he said, "I decided that…I would work on getting back at the system. Revenge."

When his bombs successfully killed and maimed the people he targeted, Kaczynski demonstrated a complete lack of remorse. He was so cut off from his own humanity that he was incapable of identifying with others. In his last attack, on April 24, 1995, Kaczynski mailed a bomb to William Dennison at the California Forestry Association in Sacramento, killing lobbyist Gilbert Murray. "We have no regret about the fact that our bomb blew up the 'wrong' man," he said in a letter to the New York Times. Again, when Uranus eclipses the Sun, there is no longer a personal self or a personal other. This is eerily demonstrated in Kaczynski's use of the pronoun "we" in reference to himself, as if he has become identified with a group consciousness. His inability to experience a personal connection is evident in the cold detachment he felt toward those he killed.

There is a bitter irony to Kaczynski's admission that he felt no regret for killing the "wrong" man, for the wrong man was wrong in more ways than one. Kaczynski never knew the war he was fighting was with himself.

---

* Note that the signs that Sun and Uranus rule, Leo and Aquarius, are actually opposed one another in the natural zodiac. Accordingly, regardless of any actual aspect between Sun and Uranus, their essential relationship is oppositional.

The Reactionary

Another variation on the theme of the unintegrated Sun-Uranus aspect is the reactionary—someone radically opposed to progress and liberalism and, by definition, all things Uranian. Certainly Kaczynski exemplifies this theme. Whereas Rodman identified with the Uranian impulse and struggled against his solar ego (he had to kill the conformist in himself), here we have the opposite: the solar ego struggling against the Uranian drive, and finally becoming possessed by it. A good example is would-be reform party presidential candidate, Pat Buchanan (Sun opposition Uranus), who is renowned for his strident conservatism and rabid Republicanism—so rabid, in fact, that he has been branded as too conservative for his own party (hence his reform party candidacy).

Note that "reform" is a Uranian word. That Buchanan has now become identified with "reformers" exemplifies what Jung called *enantiodromia,* the tendency for things to revert to their opposites when they become too one-sided. In his fury to defend the status quo against radicals, Buchanan has himself become one—a shrill voice on the fringe that few take seriously. Many regard his policy of isolationism in an era of global politics as bizarre. Called "Crackpot Pat" for his defense of Hitler and soft-on-Nazism views, Buchanan has become a radical conservative, a contradiction that aptly expresses the lack of integration between his Sun and Uranus.

Fear of change is a natural consequence of the Sun's resistance to Uranus. Tompkins captures the essence of this: "It may seem that the Sun-Uranus person wants to introduce changes all over the place, which is often the case in the outer world. But on a more personal level, Sun-Uranus is, I suggest, very frightened of change."[66] This fear is not only of changes in one's environment, but, as Kaczynski demonstrated, fear that others are trying to change one's very identity—i.e., one's thoughts, values, and convictions.

If this fear is strong enough, it can be converted into zealous devotion to a cause that the individual seeks to advance with fanatical fervor. In other words, the person becomes what he fears the most: someone who tries to overpower your mind. As Winston Churchill once quipped, "A fanatic is one who can't change his mind and won't change the subject." Pat Buchanan's former role in the television show, *Crossfire*, in which he was the impassioned champion of conservative values, provides a good example of the Sun-Uranus fanatic. As Washington Irving once said, "[he was one of those] furious zealots who blow the bellows of faction until the whole furnace of politics is red-hot." Anyone who has witnessed Buchanan's rancorous style of debate will know what Irving meant.

Fear of change is also evident in Slobadan Milosevic (square), the Serb tyrant who refused to allow various sectors of Yugoslavia—Croatia, Bosnia, and Kosovo—the freedom to be self-governing. We see it again in the former Grand Wizard of the Klu Klux Klan, David Duke (conjunction), who opposed desegregation and racial equality in Louisiana. Former Governor of Alabama, George Wallace (opposition), became infamous in 1963 for defying a federal court-ordered integration of Alabama schools. Wallace actually attempted to bar the entrance of black students at the University of Alabama by standing at the doors. Again, fear of change is likewise obvious in Ted Kaczynski who was so threatened by technological progress that he waged a one-man war against it.

In each of the above cases, the Sun is resisting the Uranian principle of change, freedom, and progress until, ultimately, it becomes possessed by it. Yet, the possession is not integration, but reactionary radicalism. Whereas Rodman's reaction formation exemplified an over-identification with Uranus and a suppression of the Sun, here we have an over-identification with the Sun and a resistance to Uranus. The person appears to espouse revolutionary (Uranian) ideals, but they are unconscious and corrupted by an over-attachment to a narrow, parochial identity—e.g., Buchanan's isolationist movement becomes the US *against* the rest of the world, Miloscevic's cause was Serbia *against* the Kosovars, Duke and Wallace championed whites *against* blacks, and Kaczynski defended personal liberties *against* the proliferation of technology. This is not true altruism. It is hostility toward that which threatens the stability of one's own fragile identity.

INTEGRATION OF SUN AND URANUS

Conscious Evolution

While aspects between the Sun and Uranus represent a fundamental, archetypal challenge, the gifts that accrue from their integration are considerable. Chief among these is ability for conscious evolution, which is the conscious intent to collaborate with an evolutionary process inherent within Nature and the Universe. At a strictly solar level, this intention is relatively absent, for the ego does not consciously seek change, but validation. On the other hand, Uranus seeks change whether the individual wills it or not.

To the extent that one is preoccupied with gaining validation, Uranus will cause changes that seem against one's will, i.e., experiences that are disruptive, shocking, upsetting, and the like. However, if the individual consciously recognizes and accepts the inevitability of change and, more so, sees change as something of value, then there is greater resilience, equanimity, and openness to the unexpected. Rather than resisting change, there is the capacity to say "I *choose* this."

Conscious evolution means establishing a partnership with the Universal tendency toward growth and wholeness. This, in turn, bolsters our capacity for right action. According to Jean Klein, a contemporary master of Advaita Vedanta, right action does not come from the personality, but springs from the situation itself—from the whole.[67] When the ego does not dictate action, or strictly speaking, *reaction*, the person finds him or herself completely adequate to the situation.

Very often the intuition of right action is not pleasant for the self-image, which, feeling threatened, doubts or quarrels with the spontaneous intuition. It takes courage for the abdication of the will to happen. Yet, action that springs from global awareness of a situation is automatically right action because it is free from egoic intention. Right or correct action does not refer to a psychological state, a morality, but to function inspired directly by the situation. Such action, says Klein, is always spontaneous.

Personality Attributes

The means of right action was described by *I Ching* expert, Carol Anthony, as a willingness to be led by the higher power. Anthony, who has Uranus trine Sun in the 11th, emphasized the importance of maintaining "conscious innocence," i.e., a humble trust in the zig-zag workings of the Creative and a willingness to let go of attachment to preferred outcomes. Similarly, the Buddhist concept of *non-attachment* and the Taoist concept of *wu-wei* counsel one to act in harmony with nature. In other words, be resilient, open to change, and willing to allow things to work out without interfering in the natural course of events.

Note the difference in the above statements between solar willing and Uranian willing. In the former, the individual intends for something to happen; in the later, there is a willingness to accept those things that one cannot control. When the Sun and Uranus are integrated, one of the most salient attributes is equanimity—one of the ten *paramitas* or perfections of Buddhism. The person appears calm, cool, and collected, especially in response to events that might seem disturbing to others. A Buddhist who cultivates equanimity remains unperturbed in the face of an increasingly broad range of experience. Of such a person it is said:

> Pleasure-pain
> praise and blame
> fame and shame
> loss and gain
> are all the same.

Conversely, when Uranus and the Sun are not integrated, there is agitation, impatience, and bad temper. The person is more likely to either resist or force change, or use coercive tactics in pushing for outcomes that are preferred—like when Rodman head-butted the referee in a basketball game because things weren't going his way. The importance of equanimity in the Western tradition is perhaps best expressed in the serenity prayer.

> **God**
> grant me the
> **Serenity**
> To accept those things
> I cannot change...
> **Courage**
> to change
> the things I can
> and **Wisdom**
> to know
> the difference.

In addition to equanimity, there are a number of other attributes that result from an integration of the Sun and Uranus. While ethicality and truthfulness generally belong to the Sagittarian domain, these qualities have an Aquarian meaning as well. The Uranian archetype of the Wise Fool, for example, symbolizes a willingness to speak the truth regardless of the consequences.

This is not really done foolishly, of course, for the Fool is wise in ways that circumvent the usual defenses of the ego. There is, in other words, a healthy irreverence toward propriety, image, and pretensions of self-importance. The Fool is free of attachments that cloud perception. Distorting reality merely to protect one's own or other's self-esteem is no longer an option. The individual recognizes that lying reinforces greed, fear, guilt and other disruptive emotions. Conversely, truthfulness and ethical behavior frees the mind of guilt and fear of discovery, and consequently reduces agitation and worry.

This point is admirably illustrated in a fairy tale by Hans Christian Anderson, *The Emperor's New Clothes*. As the story goes, the emperor was so excessively fond of new clothes that he neglected his duty of caring for the people. In other words, we have a narcissist who is hung up on appearances. The emperor gets his comeuppance, however, when two swindlers come to town and offer to weave His Highness some stunning new garments. The catch, however, is that the swindlers claim that the clothes are invisible to every person who is not fit for the office he holds, or who is impossibly stupid.

Recall that the solar ego maintains self-esteem by excluding from awareness those thoughts, feelings, and impulses that it perceives as threatening to the current regime. In other words, the ego contains a large measure of self-deception. When the emperor could not see the clothes, he suspected the weavers were lying, but could not admit it for fear that he might be wrong. If others could see the clothes, he worried that they would conclude that he was either stupid or unfit for the office of emperor. In truth, he *was* unfit, but for precisely the reason that he could not see or tell the truth: *his overweening pride*.

To the extent that the emperor was ruled by pride, he was vulnerable to flattery and sycophancy, i.e., he could be deceived. On a solar-ego level, this is true for all of us. The ego hears and sees only what contributes to its inherent vanity. Its attachment to being liked predisposes it to insincerity; we become swindlers with ulterior motives—or, vulnerable to same.*

Eventually everyone realized that the weavers were imposters, but not before the King walked naked through town in a lavish procession in his honor. In short, the emperor was a victim of his own narcissism. The Uranus figure in the tale, of course, is an innocent child. "But he's got nothing on," said the child, and soon all the people were echoing the child because he was honest. This guileless and unpretentious child, who had no office to lose and was not attached to being smart, was capable of saying what no one else could. The child simply acted spontaneously. "Conscious innocence," as Anthony reminds us, requires letting oneself be an instrument of a higher power.

This Uranian virtue of spontaneous honesty is illustrated in a tale by the German mystic, Meister Eckhart, who meets a beautiful naked boy.

> The Meister asks the boy where he came from. "I come from God," says the boy. Where did you leave him? "In virtuous hearts." Where are you going? "To God." Who are you? "A King." Where is your kingdom? "In my heart." Take care that no one divide it with you! says the Meister. "I shall." The Meister leads him to his home and offers him a coat. "Then I should be no King!" says the boy, and he disappears. For it was God himself—Who was having a bit of fun.[68]

I found this charming story a rather interesting example of an integrated Sun-Uranus aspect, for two themes run through it: (1) the solar theme that kingliness is to be found in a virtuous heart;

---

* As a Sun sign Leo, President Obama has been ridiculed for his allegedly naive faith that friendliness toward middle eastern foes, e.g., Iran, would transform them into friends. This, his opponents argue, has rendered the president vulnerable to deception.

and (2) the Uranian theme that Godliness is equivalent to naked honesty. In other words, both God and nobility reside in a virtuous heart, which is at all times guileless and truthful.

Renunciation is yet another attribute that seems to accompany a healthy Sun-Uranus balance. This does not mean the relinquishment of pleasure or ambition, but a de-emphasis upon those pursuits that distract one from what is truly important: the cultivation of wisdom and love. Rather than focusing on one's own self-aggrandizement and egoistic satisfaction, greater pleasure is found in a deepening sensitivity to the moment-to-moment flow of experience.

To the extent that one masters renunciation, there is correspondingly greater freedom from attachment or aversion, and therefore less inclination to covet, grasp after, or avoid any experience. Again, Meister Eckhart said it best. "Truly I am so happy with all God does, whether he gives or withholds, that there is not a cent's worth of difference between my condition and the best I could imagine for myself."

Renunciation also confers patience, for impatience reflects dissatisfaction with present experience and attachment to preferred experience. Remember, intentionality by definition means attachment to a preferred outcome. To the extent that one is attached, there is agitation and anxiety about the future, and thus an inability to enjoy the present moment. Conversely, renunciation is based upon a trust that, in the long term, the Universe is unfolding exactly as it should, and that all things work together for the greater good. One can, therefore, afford to be patient. As the Buddha put it, "At the end of the way is freedom. Till then, patience."

If one can accept the present moment as it is, one can also accept others as they are. Patience, in this sense, means a kind of nonjudgmental acceptance and tolerance of human foibles. Thus, integration of the Sun and Uranus also enables one to be patient with others. The Sun confers the ability to prize the person, while Uranus liberates the potential to love without attachment or personal agenda. Again, one is less driven by egocentric motives. A spontaneous generosity and loving kindness emerges for its own sake, and in such a way as to most effectively serve and contribute to the collective good.

Radical Teachers

Earlier, I mentioned how a lack of integration between Sun and Uranus can result in a weak, unstable sense of self, which may lead to a compensatory grandiosity and narcissistic self-inflation. Such a person may evidence a pseudo-altruism in that his self-concept is derived more or less wholly from identification with some fanatical cause.

A good example here is David Koresh, who had Sun conjunct Uranus in the 11th with both planets squaring Jupiter in Scorpio. Koresh was the deluded, messianic leader of the infamous Branch Davidians, an apocalyptic group of religious fanatics in Waco Texas who were torched by the FBI in a tragic fire in 1993. Koresh claimed a number of divine revelations, including being told that he was a second intercessor for mankind and that Christ had only died for those *before* his crucifixion. For those that died after Christ's crucifixion, Koresh was the divine intercessor. Ultimately Koresh claimed that he was, in fact, the Son of God and that all woman (and young girls) in the group belonged to him. This meant that only *he* had the right to procreate. Talk about inflation!

If the Sun and Uranus are truly integrated and the individual is reasonably healthy, then a psychological paradox emerges: the stronger one's self-love the more one is compelled to act altruistically. In other words, the attainment of healthy self-esteem naturally predisposes one to be genuinely concerned about the welfare of others. Self-esteem enables one to act altruistically precisely because it mediates the fear that by giving oneself to a larger cause one might become engulfed by collective energies. If one has a strong sense of self, then one can afford to set oneself aside in the interest of others because there is trust that one can find one's way back home (to Self).

Otherwise, as in the case of Koresh, one's sense of self can become inflated to compensate for a fear of being eclipsed by the collective—or, stated another way, Uranus appropriates the self so that the person becomes possessed by collective energies with often disastrous consequences. In fact, both are true. The individual simultaneously evidences narcissistic self-inflation (Sun) *and* radical devotion to an irrational albeit humanitarian cause (Uranus). It's as if each planet is affected by the other yet also pushes against the other, such that each planetary principle is strained and overfunctioning to maintain itself. Thus there is a reciprocal influence combined with a mutual antagonism. The more the Sun resists the pull of Uranus, the more it becomes an exaggerated and bloated version of the solar principle. Likewise, the more Uranus resists the edict of the Sun, the more it becomes an extreme, excessive version of itself. At the same time, each planet's behavior is colored by an unavoidable and inextricable involvement with its challenger.

One way or the other, the Sun has to accommodate itself to Uranus. Healthy integration enables one to identify with the Cosmic Will, which constitutes a supreme intelligence and evolutionary purpose that transcends the individual. Yet, the person retains a realistic, grounded sense of self. In fact, integration of Uranus allows one to gain perspective —"I'm part of a larger whole (humanity)"— and humility, "I'm imperfect and subordinate to a higher power (God)." Recognizing this, the native humbly dedicates himself not only to personal growth but to global transformation. He evidences a strong but peaceful intention to implement change, especially in situations that have become stagnant.

A related theme is helping people adapt to changes, i.e., to become more resilient, open, and accommodating to collective trends that are personally or socially destabilizing. This, in effect, is the antithesis (and antidote) to the reactionary who capitalizes on people's fear of change. I know of one client who had Sun square Uranus that gave a public lecture titled "Living In Times of Accelerated Change". She also gave workshops to corporations that needed help in coping with the effect of technological and social changes on the workplace.

Sun-Uranus individuals may feel a sense of purpose to awaken others to new possibilities, to advance radical new ideas, and to function as a trailblazer and spokesperson for progress. Changes advocated typically reflect Uranian themes of human rights, social reform, and world unity. Spiritual teachers such as Ram Dass, Timothy Leary, Carol Anthony, Rudolph Steiner, Krishnamurti, Jean Houston, and Marianne Williamson—all of whom have their Sun in close aspect to Uranus—are exemplars of such ideals.

Innovative Artists

If the Sun is creativity, and Uranus is about revelation, then integration of these two functions allows for creative expression that startles, reveals, and enlightens. A good example here is Colin Higgins (Sun sextile Uranus), who wrote the screenplay for the delightfully original film, *Harold and Maude*. Virtually every scene in the film is a revelation of one sort or another, and the viewer cannot help but feel transported to a higher level of awareness. Robert Bly (square), author, poet, and exponent of the "Wild Man" archetype as articulated in his best selling book, *Iron John*, also exemplifies the originality and brilliance that comes from integration of these two functions.

Sun-Uranus creativity is not meant simply to entertain, but to awaken. Consider, for example, two controversial films of Oliver Stone (square), *Born on The 4th of July* and *Platoon*, both of which awakened people to the horrors of the Vietnam War. Indeed, *Born on The 4th of July* was a saga about a real-life Vietnam vet, Ron Kovic, who joined the Marines as a gung-ho recruit in the 1960s and came home paralyzed from the chest down—only to endure an even greater ordeal of physical and mental rehabilitation before emerging as an anti-war activist. It's also a story about one man's personal odyssey and path to enlightenment. Kovic changes from a boozing, quarrelsome, insufferable U.S. loyalist who is contemptuous of war protesters, until he suddenly "wakes up" and realizes they are right. He takes up the banner of the Vietnam Veterans Against the War and emerges as a true hero in his address at the 1976 Democratic convention.

Stone's movie is not simply about battle or wounds or recovery, but about an American who changes his mind about the war and then changes the minds of millions of other Americans. Awakening, revelation, social activism, championing a cause, heroism, change—these are classic Sun-Uranus themes. In addition to *4th of July* and *Platoon*, Stone's film, *JFK*, was likewise a startling revelation of the complexities surrounding the assassination of President Kennedy.

Stephen Spielberg (opposition) has made a number of films that deal with similar subjects, notably *Schindler's List*, which explores the conflict between self-interest (Sun) and concern for humanity at large (Uranus). *Searching for Private Ryan,* Spielberg's searing war drama, explores a related theme: Ryan's choice between self-preservation versus loyalty to the group. In both these films, we see the true Sun-Uranus Hero who is willing to dedicate himself for the benefit of the whole.

Spielberg's Space Fantasies

Sun-Uranian themes are perhaps nowhere more evident than in Spielberg's award-winning science-fiction movies, *Close Encounters of the Third Kind* and *E.T. the Extra Terrestrial*. Not only were they landmarks in the development of special effects—Uranian technology utilized for Solar creativity—but both deal with divine revelation as embodied in alien messengers from other worlds, apt symbols for the higher consciousness that Uranus represents. In each film, the main protagonist exemplifies the childlike awe and trust that is characteristic of Sun-Uranus.

In E.T. the story begins with a 10-year old boy, Elliott, who feels alienated and alone because his parents have divorced and he is separated from his father. This in itself is a Sun-Uranus theme, as discussed in my earlier commentary on Rodman. Meanwhile E.T. is an alien scientist on a research project, snuffling about the woods looking for plant specimens when suddenly humans arrive—Capricorn authorities with flashlights and big stomping boots. They close in on the spaceship and it is forced to take off and abandon E.T. Just as Elliott feels alienated from his father, so E.T. has been separated from his loved ones—a rather more serious case of "alienation".

Elliott's experience of alienation enables him to identify with the creature. He knows there is something "out there" and he sits up all night with his flashlight in hopes of discovering what it is. As the film develops, his identification with E.T. grows stronger and stronger. If Elliott signifies the Leonine hero of our story, then E.T. signifies Aquarius. Yet, each has some characteristics of the other. Elliott shows early signs of being an Aquarian "liberator" when he frees the frogs from their captive state in his biology class, whereas E.T. is all "heart"—a Leonine attribute. In fact, E.T.'s heart is central to the story, for it is disproportionately large and glows when he is possessed of strong feeling.

E.T. the Extra Terrestrial is a metaphorical enactment of the relationship between Leo and Aquarius. Spielberg's fusion of science fiction and mythology is actually a story about love, an inseparable bond between a pre-adolescent boy and a higher intelligence from outer space. As their relationship develops, E.T., who is very wise and possesses psi abilities such as psychokinesis, is able to telepathically communicate with Elliott. Eventually E.T. conveys to Elliott that he wants to go home—back to the stars. Part of the Aquarian appeal of the film is that Spielberg enables us to experience the world from an alien perspective, i.e., through E.T.'s eyes, ears, and senses. Like a Promethean figure from another galaxy, E.T. functions as a mediator between the gods and humankind.

This is symbolized near the end of the film when Elliott is left alone with E.T. to say goodbye after E.T. has apparently died. "I'll believe in you all my life, every day," says Elliott bravely. "E.T., I love you." Suddenly E.T.'s heart awakens anew, a joyous radiance of red. It is the climactic moment in the film and seems to symbolize the full awakening of Elliott's potential for altruistic love. For only when he has the courage to let go of E.T. is his potential for true heroic action revealed. For Elliott must sacrifice his attachment to E.T. by liberating him from the strictures of government authority and assisting his reunion with the aliens that have returned to take E.T. home.

This act of "altruistic love" is testimony to the integration of Sun and Uranus, and is symbolized by the scene in which Elliott and E.T. soar to both literal and poetic heights on Elliott's bicycle. Elliott learns to "let go" of E.T., and by implication his father, yet in so doing he attains something greater—a heart connection with a higher consciousness to which he will be forever linked. Just before E.T. departs, his alien heart aglow with love, he places his finger gently on Elliott's forehead. "I'll be right here" he says.

Whereas ET ends with an alien transmission from the earth to the heavens, "ET phone home," *Close Encounters* begins with an alien transmission from the heavens to the earth. Reminiscent of the Aquarian figure with the upturned urn, the main character of the film, Ray Neary (Richard Dreyfus), receives a "psychic implanting" from a higher consciousness—the UFO—that compels him to find its source. At the beginning of the film, Neary is the perfect Everyman struggling with a frustrating enigma that finally becomes clear. Once Neary realizes that he was the recipient of an alien transmission directly into his brain, he is possessed of a trust and a mission that is impossible to explain to his embattled wife. With Uranus, it is no longer about belief; one simply *knows*. It is a revelation, and it changes everything.

When Neary has his first encounter, it causes his company truck to shake—Uranus "shakes you up"— and awakens him to the fact that there are greater powers in the universe. Alien beings offer the promise of life beyond the restrictions of conventional middle-class life; the spaceships in *Close Encounters* unheedingly pass the toll booths on the state highway, markers that signify the ego boundaries of the conventional solar/Leo world.

If *ET* was a Promethean mediator between the gods and humankind, then in *Close Encounters* it was Ray Neary who served as a mediator between humankind and the gods. Again, Neary's reception of the alien transmission is reminiscent of the Aquarian symbol of the man on one knee with the upturned urn. Just as that image signifies the human capacity for channeling the universal consciousness that flows downward from heaven to earth, so Neary serves as a receptacle for the channeling of a higher intelligence—literally a cosmic mind—that flows downward from the UFO to Neary's mind. Once penetrated by that consciousness, his life changes utterly and irrevocably. Neary realizes that there is something *more* and he must find it.

Possessed of this mission, he is willing to sacrifice everything—his marriage, his family, his career, even his life. Neary is on a hero's journey. At the film's end he is chosen by the aliens to board the mother ship and be taken on a trip to the stars—back home to source—an echo of *E.T.* Neary's departure aboard the mother ship for unknown adventures is the film's final grandiloquent embrace of the possible. Just as the true hero must "bring back the boon" and share with the larger community what he has learned on his journey, so Neary will return and share with the community what he learns. Again, Aquarius signifies the completion and culmination of the Hero's Journey.*

MORE SCIENCE FICTION

I found it interesting that several other innovative film makers with Sun-Uranus aspects were also associated with science fiction movies involving alien beings. Before his dramatic arrival in Hollywood, Orson Welles (square) had carved a considerable reputation in theatre and radio as an imaginative, experimental, and technically daring genius intent on stretching existing forms beyond established limits. By concocting news bulletins and eye witness accounts that were seamlessly woven into his Halloween 1938 radio broadcast of H.G. Wells's *War of the Worlds,* Welles created a narrative so shockingly authentic that listeners actually thought New Jersey was being attacked by a vanguard of invaders from Mars.

John Sayles (square), one of America's best known independent filmmakers, was awarded a prestigious MacArthur Foundation "genius grant" in 1983. The result was *The Brother From Another Planet,* a highly original story of a mute, black alien adrift in Harlem.

---

* Speaking of "bringing back the boon," it is interesting to note that clinical psychologist Richard Boylan (Sun quincunx Uranus) has spent the last twenty years chronicling cases of clients who report positive experiences as UFO abductees. These cases are detailed in Boylan's book, *Close Extraterrestrial Encounters: Positive Experiences With Mysterious Visitors* (1994).

Because the main character cannot talk, and his instinctive response is a sort of detached Aquarian friendliness, people naturally open up to him. And since our hero has literally dropped out of the skies, he doesn't have an opinion or judgment about anything. Thus, like Sun-Uranus, he is radically open to new experience. In this way, the Brother functions as a kind of Observing Self for contemporary society, forcing us to become aware of ourselves.

Among science fiction writers, perhaps none was more widely loved and appreciated than Robert Heinlein (opposition), one of the early masters of the craft. His most famous book, *Stranger In A Strange Land*, is required reading for many U.S. high school students and elevated Heinlein as the archetypal science fiction author for an entire generation.

Stranger In A Strange Land is about Valentine Michael Smith, a human raised by Martians who comes to earth as a true innocent, having no knowledge of human culture or religion. He explores human morality and the meaning of love, and eventually starts his own religion based on "free love" — what else? *Stranger In A Strange Land* is a classic example of the alienation that the Sun-Uranus type so often feels, and in this regard parallels Sayles's *Brother From Another Planet* and Spielberg's *E.T. The Extra Terrestial*. Valentine Michael Smith has to discover what it means to be human and thus, like the observing ego, holds up a mirror in which we are able to "grok" ourselves.*

Other writers with Sun-Uranus aspects read as a veritable *Who's Who* of science fiction. Ray Bradbury (opposition) is one of the most prolific writers of science fiction this century. His most famous

---

* To grok something is to understand it so profoundly that its nature is intuitively clear to you. There are few words in English that came from an extraterrestrial source, but grok is one of them. In this case, it is from the language of fictional Martians in Heinlein's 1961 science fiction novel, "Stranger In A Strange Land." The book's main character, Michael Valentine Smith, brings the word to Earth. When Heinlein's book became popular, the word spread among young people, and today has become a well-established part of the language. Grok is a Uranian word in that it implies a realization, a flash of illumination, a wholistic intuitive understanding that enables a person to perceive a given phenomenon's inherent complexity.

book, *The Martian Chronicles,* as well as his best known short story, *R Is for Rocket,* both deal with futuristic themes about aliens and outer space. Others who have dealt with futuristic themes include George Orwell (opposition), author of *1984,* and Aldous Huxley (square), who wrote *Brave New World.*

Arthur C. Clarke (sextile), another great master of science fiction, and Stanley Kubrick (trine), the brilliant screenwriter and filmmaker, received an academy award nomination for their screenplay, *2001: A Space Odyssey*, based on one of Clarke's short stories. *2001* was an instant science-fiction classic and the quintessential late 60s "head" movie. Again, we have the motif of a "message" from a more advanced intelligence that comes "down" to earth, as symbolized by the monolith, a perfect, non-human construction. The monolith is a cosmic road sign that points beyond time and space toward the infinite potential of human evolution.

Trickster Comics

Modern day Tricksters with Sun-Uranus aspects can be found in the comedic field where much of their creativity entails an objectification and parody of the ego. Consider, for example, Steve Martin (sextile), whose early films such as *The Jerk* and *The Lonely Guy* seem to poke fun at the pretensions of the ego. Martin's "wild and crazy guy" antics in which he postures a kind of mock arrogance teach us not to take ourselves too seriously.

The same is true for nebbish Woody Allen (quincunx), a classic Fool who invites us to identify with his stumbling, cowardly, and ineffectual ways in innumerable films, the most recent of which, *Antz,* depicts him as a Trickster Hero whose utopian vision and defiance of the megalomaniacal ruler galvanizes the colony to rebellion.

Other notable examples of modern Fools with Sun-Uranus aspects are Jim Carrey, Roseanne Barr, Howard Stern, Billy Crystal, Chevy Chase, John Stewart, Bill Maher, and the late Lenny

Bruce. Often their humor is self-effacing, or there is a goofy, idiotic, silly quality to their characters, as if they are modeling humility. Carrey's film, *Dumb and Dumber,* is typical of this genre. Also remarkable is Carrey's recent depiction of the legendary comic, Andy Kaufman, in the film biography, *Man On The Moon.* Carrey and Kaufman were both born on January 17th (13 years apart), and both have an extremely close quincunx between Sun and Uranus.

Another version of the Fool is provided by Chevy Chase, who has a Sun-Uranus trine with Moon in Aquarius. In his three *National Lampoon* vacation movies, Chase plays the sweet but bumbling, ineffectual, and terminally stupid head of the household, Clark Griswold. He again plays the Trickster in *Fletch* where his character has a penchant for goofy disguises (remember the Trickster is a transformer and symbolizes the multiplicity of consciousness).

I found it interesting that film reviewer, Roger Ebert, criticized Chase's performance in *Fletch* for "his monotone, deadpan cynicism, [and for] distancing himself from the material."[69] Yet, Chase's deadpan humor is understandable given his Sun trine Uranus and Aquarian Moon. Uranus/Aquarius, of course, is the observing ego, the witness, the watcher on the hills that perceives the world from a distance. Not realizing the astrological significance of his remarks, Ebert gives us a pretty good description: "The problem is, Chase projects such an inflexible mask of cool detachment, of ironic running commentary, that we're prevented from identifying with him. If he thinks this is all just a little too silly for words, what are we to think?"[70]

Brilliant Thinkers

One of Uranus' key processes is that of discovery and invention, which seems to flow from a particular kind of mind-set: the ability to perceive wholes, an understanding of complexity and interdependency, non-dualistic thinking, and an emphasis on change (impermanence). In addition, Uranian cognition is radically objective and intuitive, i.e., capable of direct, immediate apprehension that transcends linear thought—like the psychic implanting in *Close Enounters*. If the Sun is the creative impulse, then Sun-Uranus aspects appear to correlate with that "flash of genius" which is the progenitor of creative, original discoveries.

In his book, *Prometheus the Awakener*, Richard Tarnas (trine) first identifies the Greek titan Prometheus as a Uranian archetype and then cites historical Promethean figures that are exemplars of Sun-Uranus aspects. These include the chief protagonists of the Scientific Revolution—Copernicus, Kepler, Galileo, Descartes, and Newton—as well as the founding revolutionaries of modern philosophy—John Locke and Emmanuel Kant—and two of the founding revolutionaries of modern psychology, Sigmund Freud and William James.

Kant (opposition) is particularly noteworthy in that his 1781 landmark work, *Critique of Pure Reason*, established two imperatives of human understanding. First, the knower participates in that which he knows. Second, our minds not only conform to reality, but reality—the objects themselves—conform to our way of knowing. In other words, Kant was sufficiently objective to recognize that a completely objective description of reality is impossible. For every act of perception is unavoidably mediated by our own subjective structures—ideas, beliefs, assumptions, and expectations. What we know and experience, therefore, is to an indeterminate extent a projection of our own minds.

The same point was made two centuries later by Werner Heisenberg (conjunction), one of the chief architects of the new physics. Heisenberg's "indeterminacy principal" established that the results of an experiment are determined as much by the experimental set-up and by the expectations of the observer, as they are by the events themselves. What "happens" in a given experiment, says

Heisenberg "depends on our way of observing it, or on the fact that we observe it."[71] Thus, like Kant, he concludes, "we do not study nature herself, but nature exposed to our method of questioning."[72]

A contemporary scientist that exemplifies Sun-Uranus is the physicist-author, Fritjof Capra (square), whose landmark book, *The Tao of Physics,* explored the striking parallels between modern physics and eastern mysticism. Capra's work concentrates on two ideas that are classic examples of Sun-Uranus perception: (1) the unity and interrelation of all things and events, and (2) the intrinsically dynamic nature of the universe. The first emphasizes the concept of *wholeness,* and the second of *impermanence.*

According to Capra, quantum theory reveals the essential interconnectedness of the universe. Rather than depicting the universe as a billiard table of colliding atoms, which was the dominant metaphor of Newtonian mechanics, quantum physics conceives the universe as a unified web of interrelated energy patterns in an ongoing dynamic process. Particles, if they exist at all, must be regarded as composite structures wherein every particle helps to generate other particles, which, in turn, generate it. Accordingly, it is no longer possible to reduce the world into independently existing smallest units because these alleged units are merely patterns of probable interconnections such that "every particle consists of all other particles."[73]

> Quantum theory forces us to see the universe not as a collection of physical objects, but rather as a complicated web of relations between the various parts of a unified whole.[74]

This perception of ultimate reality as an unbroken whole in flowing movement was also described by Werner Heisenberg:

> The world thus appears as a complicated tissue of events, in which connections of different kinds alternate or overlap or combine and thereby determine the texture of the whole.[75]

In modern physics, mass is no longer associated with a material substance. Particles are seen as bundles of energy that flow into one another, like two clouds mixing. Capra reminds us, however, that energy "is associated with activity, with processes, and this implies that the nature of subatomic particles is intrinsically dynamic." The word "dynamic" means "characterized by continuous change, activity, or progress." All of this, of course, constitutes Capra's second fundamentally Uranian perception, namely that the most basic property of the universe is change, or impermanence.

Both Heisenberg and Capra emphasize that one of the most startling developments in modern physics is that ultimate reality transcends ordinary language, logic, and concepts. The same is true of mysticism. Capra states it thusly:

> Both the physicist and the mystic want to communicate their knowledge, and when they do so with words their statements are paradoxical and full of logical contradictions. These paradoxes are characteristic of all mysticism, from Heraclitus to Don Juan, and since the beginning of this century they are also characteristic of physics.[76]

In *Part I*, I mentioned how the Taoist concept of *wu wei* describes a way of harmonizing with ultimate reality. But *wu wei* is innately paradoxical, being defined as "effortless effort," "non-doing," "the secret of action without deeds," and "actionless activity." Likewise in subatomic physics we are confronted with such paradoxical entities as "massless particles" and electrons that are both wave *and* particle. When Heisenberg founded one of the most important principles of quantum theory—the uncertainty principle—he established in formal terms the paradoxical nature of subatomic reality.

Recall that a paradox derives from an assertion that is self-contradictory, yet at a higher level of understanding emerges as true.

Accordingly, to understand a paradox I have to elevate my perception to a level that transcends the opposing ideas. Paradox is a property of perceiving things holistically, or non-dualistically, such that ultimate reality is conceptualized as a unification of opposites. Again, this type of creative perception and discovery is typical of Sun-Uranus.

An example of paradoxical thinking in the medical field is that of Jonas Salk (square), the American physician who discovered the cure for polio. Despite the doubts of his colleagues, Salk intuited that a vaccine against polio could be developed from the polio virus itself. His radical, paradoxical discovery—preventing polio by injecting polio into the human subject—earned him the Congressional Gold Medal for Great Achievement in the field of medicine.

In the field of psychiatry, Dr. Milton Erikson (conjunction), who was born the same day as Heisenberg, developed a new, radical technique that came to be known as paradoxical psychotherapy. Made famous in a book by Jay Haley, *Uncommon Therapy*, which subsequently became an entirely new school of therapy, Erikson's methods involved placing the patient in a double-bind by prescribing the very symptoms that motivated her to seek help. This, of course, is analogous to Salk's injection of the polio virus as a cure for polio. In other words, Erikson's use of paradox in his therapeutic interventions is the psychiatric equivalent to the paradoxical formulations of Salk in medicine and Heisenberg in physics.

Heroic Revolutionaries

The final word on Sun-Uranus aspects is the heroic revolutionary. In this category are those individuals who, unlike their reactionary counterparts, support social or political revolutions that are characterized by true, humanitarian ideals. The Sun provides the heroic impulse, whereas Uranus provides the vision and impetus to dedicate oneself to the collective good. Perhaps no one said it better than Thomas Jefferson (square), who penned the Declaration of Independence that catalyzed the American Revolution.

> We hold these truths to be self-evident, that all men are created equal, that they are endowed by their Creator with certain unalienable Rights, that among these are Life, Liberty and the pursuit of Happiness.

Jefferson was a true revolutionary and epitomized the broad, detached perspective typical of a Sun-Uranus aspect. In 1787, when he was in Paris and heard about Daniel Shays's rebellion of poor farmers in Massachusetts, Jefferson was the only American leader *not* alarmed by news of the revolt. In a letter to James Madison, he wrote: "I hold it that a little rebellion, now and then, is a good thing, and as necessary in the political world as storms in the physical...It is a medicine necessary for the sound health of government." Later that year, and in reference to the same rebellion, he wrote: "What signify a few lives lost in a century or two? The tree of liberty must be refreshed from time to time with the blood of patriots and tyrants. It is its natural manure."

Jefferson's sentiments no doubt would have struck a chord with a few 20th century revolutionaries. Abbie Hoffman (quincunx), for example, the wildly creative and iconoclastic founder of Yippies (Youth International Party), wrote *Revolution For The Hell Of It* and was one of the Chicago Seven arrested for conspiracy to bring down the government in 1968. Hoffman was a radical and activist from his UC Berkeley days in the 1960's when he opposed the Vietnam War. He was arrested for the 42nd time in 1987 while protesting CIA recruitment at the University of Massachusetts.

Johan Raskin, his biographer, recalls that Hoffman constantly reinvented his own identity, believing that "reality is made up," echoing a statement by Trudy, the Trickster bag lady. "Abbie just had this ironic sense of self, of making fun of himself," Raskin said. Calling him "the last genuine American revolutionary," Raskin states: "He wasn't connected with any organization, he never had a 9-to-5 job, but he had a calling and a vocation—to make people aware of the world in which they were living, and to do something about it."[77]

There are other revolutionaries, of course, that typify the Sun-Uranus aspect. Rita Mae Brown (opposition), the American author of *Rubyfruit Jungle* and *Southern Discomfort* was active in the civil rights movement and an open lesbian feminist. Another radical feminist, Germaine Greer (square), wrote the 1970 best selling book, *The Female Eunuch*, which ignited flames of rebellion in millions of women around the world, eventually being translated into 12 languages. Twenty years later, and still echoing the concerns of her generation, Greer wrote *The Change: Women, Aging and Menopause.* Note that the title and subject of the book is Uranian, *Change.*

Malcolm X (sextile), the brilliant leader and spokesperson for the Black Muslim movement in the 1960's, worked tirelessly to build black pride and inspire hope that all races might someday be joined in brotherhood. Another black leader, political activist Huey Newton (square), co-founded the Black Panthers, which was a symbol of black militancy in the mid-60s and early 70s. Of course, whether these men are heroic revolutionaries or merely political anarchists depends on one's point of view.

Few of us will question the heroic revolutionary status of our final example, Nelson Mandela (quincunx), the elder statesman of the black liberation movement in South Africa. Mandela spent his entire life fighting racial oppression. After being imprisoned for 27 years, he emerged as a symbol of everything unjust about South Africa's racially discriminatory laws. Mandela was considered the one man who could bridge the vast divide between whites and blacks. A charismatic hero (Sun), he also represented sacrifice for the cause of democracy (Uranus). On May 2, 1994, he claimed victory for the African National Congress when he was elected the first black president of South Africa.

SUMMARY

We have seen that there are myriad ways in which the archetypal blend of Sun-Uranus aspects can be expressed. As is true for any aspect, these planetary energies operate on a continuum of integration. At one extreme are the personality disorders that typify this combination—identity disorder, schizoid disorder, and narcissistic inflation characterized by erratic ungrounded behavior, egocentric radicalism, and pretensions of enlightenment. Such people have problems with change, either being afraid of it (the reactionary) or becoming so identified with revolution that they evidence impatience and hostility toward those who resist it.

At the other extreme are those rare individuals who have achieved a balance between Solar and Uranian dimensions of the psyche. Such people tend to be proponents of conscious evolution. They embody ethicality, truthfulness, humility, Buddhist non-attachment, equanimity when faced with threats to stability, and patience in the face of obstacles that retard progress. Exemplars of change in the most positive sense, these people are the true spokespersons for progressive reform, human rights, and world peace. Internal self-revelation is balanced by a commitment to social revolution.

Sun-Uranus creativity can take a variety of forms, from entertainment that enlightens, to science fiction that provides us with a glimpse of our possible future. Trickster comics teach us to not take ourselves too seriously, and that our current identities are but way stations on a journey toward emancipation from the dictates of ego.

Aspects between Sun and Uranus also frequently show up in the charts of brilliant thinkers whose discoveries remind us that progress is both necessary and inevitable. Other exemplars of integrated Sun-Uranus aspects are heroic revolutionaries who champion the cause of liberty and lead the fight against oppression and tyranny.

Radical teachers such as Jidu Krishnamurti, Baba Ram Dass, and Jean Houston help us to see that self-realization is a prelude to global transformation. Perhaps it is fitting to end with the words of Marianne Williamson (Sun-Uranus conjunction), an American visionary at the forefront of the human potential movement. Her words seem singularly capable of conveying the meaning of a fully integrated Sun-Uranus aspect.

> Our deepest fear is not that we are inadequate.
>
> Our deepest fear is that we are powerful beyond measure.
>
> It is our light, not our darkness, that most frightens us.
>
> We ask ourselves, who am I to be brilliant, gorgeous, talented and fabulous?
>
> Actually, who are you not to be?
>
> You are a child of God. Your playing small doesn't serve the world.
>
> There's nothing enlightened about shrinking so that other people won't feel insecure around you.
>
> We were born to make manifest the glory of God that is within us.
>
> It's not just in some of us; it's in everyone. And as we let our own light shine, we unconsciously give other people permission to do the same.
>
> As we are liberated from our own fear, our presence automatically liberates others.[78]

* * *

ENDNOTES

1. Erikson, E., *Childhood and society*. New York: Norton., 1963
2. Perry, G., *Mapping the Landscape of the Soul*. San Rafael, CA: AAP Press, 2012
3. Rosenberg, S., *Conceiving the self*. New York: Basic Books, 1979
4. Hales, S., *Understanding the nature of self-esteem*. The Saybrook Perspective. 3, 3-17, 1987, p. 5
5. Ibid., p. 4
6. Suzuki, D.T., *The essence of Buddhism*. Kyoto, Japan: Hozokan, 1968, p. 33
7. Bruteau, B., *Evolution toward divinity*. Wheaton, IL: Theosophical Publishing House, 1974
8. Anthony, C., *A guide to the I Ching*. Stow, MA: Anthony Publishing Company, 1981, p. 34
9. Hall, M.P., *The essential nature of consciousness*. Los Angeles: Philosophical Research Society, 1954, p. 1
10. Ibid., p. 8
11. Chapple, C., *Karma and creativity*. Albany, NY: State University of New York Press 1986; Creel, A.B., In defense of karma and rebirth: Evolutionary karma. In R.W. Neufeldt (Ed.), *Karma and rebirth* (pp. 15-40). Albany, NY: State University of New York Press, 1986
12. Smith, H., *Forgotten truth: The primordial tradition*. New York: Harper & Row,1976
13. Aurobindo, S., *Birth centenary library*. Pondicheery: Sri Aurobindo Ashram Press 1972
14. Creel, *Karma and rebirth*, p. 10
15. Taylor, E., Asian Interpretations: Transcending the stream of consciousness. In K. Pope & J. Singer (Eds.), *The stream of consciousness*. New York: Plenum Press, 1978, p. 36
16. Deikman, A.J., *The observing self*. Boston: Beacon Press, 1982
17. Anthony, C.K., *A guide to the I Ching*. Stow, MA: Anthony Publishing Company, 1988, p. x
18. Ibid.
19. Hales, *Understanding the nature of self-esteem*, 1987
20. Cialdini, R.B., Darby, B.L, & Vincent, Y.E., *Transgression and altruism: A case for hedonism*. Journal of Experimental Social Psychology, 9, 1973, p. 502-516
21. Jung, C.G., *The Archetypes and the Collective Unconscious*. Collected Works, Vol. 9 (1), Bollingen Series XX. New York: Pantheon, 1959
22. May, R., *Love and will*. New York: Norton, 1969, p. 224
23. Pearson, C., *Awakening the heroes within*. San Francisco, Ca.: Harper, 1991, p. 183
24. Whitehead, A.N., *The concept of nature*. Cambridge: Cambridge University Press, 1920
25. Griffin, D.R., God and religion in the post-modern world. Albany, NY: State University of New York Press, 1989, p. 5
26. Chapple, C., *Karma and creativity*
27. Pearson, *Awakening the heroes within*, p. 163
28. Gibran, K., *The prophet*. New York: Alfred Knopf, 1923, p. 52
29. May, R., *Love and will*. New York: Norton, 1969, p. 243
30. Ebert, R., "Star trek II: The wrath of Khan," and "Fletch," both in *Cinemania 97*, a Microsoft CD, 1997
31. Deikman, A.J., *The observing self*
32. Greene, 1996; Idemon, 1996; Sasportas, 1989; Tarnas, 1995
33. Vogler, C., *The writers journey*. Studio City, Ca.: Michael Wiese Productions, 1992, p. 89
34. Singer, J., *Boundaries of the soul*. Garden City, NY: Doubleday & Company 1972, p. 255
35. Guirand, A., "Greek Mythology," in *New Larousse encyclopedia of mythology*. New York: Hemline Publishing House, 1968, p. 94
36. Pearson, *Awakening the heroes within*, 1991
37. Ibid., p. 64
38. Ibid., p. 65

39. Ibid., p. 220
40. Willeford, W., *The Fool and his scepter: A study in clowns and jesters and their audience.* Evanston, IL: Northwestern Univ. Press, 1969, p. 155
41. Pearson, *Awakening the heroes within*, p. 221
42. Welsford, E., *The Fool: This Social and Literary History.* Garden City, NY: Doubleday, 1961, p. 327
43. Wagner, J., *The search for signs of intelligent life in the universe.* New York: Harper & Row, 1985, p. 18
44. Ibid.
45. Pearson, *Awakening the heroes within*, p. 230
46. Holt, P., "Hook Shots," in *San Francisco Chronicle,* May 6, 1997, p. E1-3 1997, p. E3
47. Cook, K., "Playboy Interview: Dennis Rodman," in *Playboy Magazine,* vol. 44, no. 6, June 1997, p. 59
48. Rodman, D., Bad as I wanna be. New York: Dell, 1996
49. Cook, K., Playboy Magazine, vol. 44, no. 6,, p. 60
50. Ibid.., 62
51. Rodman, D., *Bad as I wanna be,* p. 11
52. Stern, H., *Private parts.* New York: Pocket Books, 1993, p. 164
53. Ibid., p. 30
54. Ibid., 35
55. Ibid., 33
56. Cook, K., "Playboy Interview: Dennis Rodman," p. 62
57. Ibid., p. 171
58. Rosenfeld, S., "Bomber: A tortured individual," in *San Francisco Examiner,* Sep.13, 1998, p. B-9
59. Cruz Lat, E., "Kaczynski: Childhood of rage," in *San Francisco Examiner,* Nov. 2, 1997, p. A-11
60. Ibid.
61. Rosenfeld, S., "Bomber: A tortured individual," p. B-9
62. Ibid.
63. Kovaleski, S. "Kaczynski's letters home paint a chilling portrait," in *San Francisco Chronicle,* January 20, 1997, p. A4
64. Cruz Lat, E., "Kaczynski: Childhood of rage," p. A-11
65. Rosenfeld, S., "Bomber: A tortured individual," p. B-9
66. Tompkins, S., *Aspects in astrology.* Rockport, Ma.: Element Books, 1989, p. 113
67. Klein, J., *Ease of being.* New York: Norton, 1988
68. Sohhl, R. and Carr, A., (eds) *The Gospel According to Zen,* New York: Mentor Books. 1970.
69. Ebert, R., Cinemania 97, p.1
70. Ibid.
71. Heisenberg, W., *Physics and philosophy.* New York: Harper & Row, 1958, p. 50
72. Ibid., p. 54
73. Capra, F., "Modern physics and eastern mysticism," *Journal of Transpersonal Psychology,* 8, 20-40, 1976, p. 37
74. Ibid., p. 23
75. Heisenberg, W., *Physics and philosophy* 1958, p. 96
76. Capra, F., *The Tao of physics.* Berkeley: Shabhala. 1975, p. 46
77. Berkofsky, J. "Yiddishe Yippie's life bared in biography," in Jewish Bulletin of Northern California, San Francisco Jewish Community Publications Inc., 1997
78. Williamson, W., *A return to love: Reflections on the principles of a course in miracles.* New York: Harper Collins, 1996

REFERENCES

Anthony, C. K. (1981). *The philosophy of the I Ching*. Stow, MA: Anthony Publishing Company

Anthony, C. K. (1981). *A guide to the I Ching*. Stow, MA: Anthony Publishing Company

Aurobindo, S. (1972). *Birth centenary library*. Pondicheery: Sri Aurobindo Ashram Press

Bergson, H. (1964). *Creative evolution*. (A. Mitchell, trans.). London: Macmillan

Berkofsky, J. (1997). "Yiddishe Yippie's life bared in biography," in *Jewish Bulletin of Northern California,* San Francisco Jewish Community Publications Inc.

Bruteau, B. (1974). *Evolution toward divinity*. Wheaton, IL: Theosophical Publishing House.

Campbell, J. (1949). *The hero with a thousand faces*. New York: Bollingen Foundation

Capra, F. (1975). *The Tao of physics*. Berkeley: Shabhala.

Capra, F. (1976). "Modern physics and eastern mysticism," *Journal of Transpersonal Psychology*, 8, 20-40

Chapple, C. (1986). *Karma and creativity*. Albany, NY: State University of New York Press

Cialdini, R.B., Darby, B.L, & Vincent, Y.E. (1973). *Transgression and altruism: A case for hedonism.* Journal of Experimental Social Psychology, 9, 502-516

Cook, K. (1997) "Playboy Interview: Dennis Rodman," in *Playboy Magazine,* vol. 44, no. 6, June 1997

Creel, A.B. (1986). In defense of karma and rebirth: Evolutionary karma. In R.W. Neufeldt (Ed.), *Karma and rebirth* (pp. 15-40). Albany, NY: State University of New York Press

Cruz Lat, E. (1997). "Kaczynski: Childhood of rage," in *San Francisco Examiner,* Nov. 2, 1997, p. A-ll. de Silva, P. (1981).

de Silva, P. (1981). Two paradigmatic strands in the Buddhist theory of consciousness. In R. Valle & R. von Eckartsberg (Eds.), *The metaphors of Consciousness* (pp. 275-286). New York: Plenum Press.

Deci, E. (1975). *Intrinsic motivation.* New York: hell Plenum.

Deikman, A.J. (1982). *The observing self.* Boston: Beacon Press

Ebert, R. (1997). "Star trek II: The wrath of Khan," and "Fletch," both in *Cinemania 97*, a Microsoft CD.

Engel, L. (1990). *Imaginary crimes.* Boston: Houghton Miffin.

Erikson, E. (1963). *Childhood and society.* New York: Norton

Gibran, K. (1923). *The prophet.* New York: Alfred Knopf

Gootnik, E. (1997). *Why you behave in ways you hate.* Granite Bay, CA: Penmarin Books

Griffin, D.R. (1989). *God and religion in the post-modern world.* Albany, NY: State University of New York Press

Guirand, A. (1968). "Greek Mythology," in *New Larousse encyclopedia of mythology.* New York: Hemline Publishing House

Greene, L. (1996). *The art of stealing fire.* London: CPA Press

Hales, S. (1987). *Understanding the nature of self-esteem.* The Saybrook Perspective. 3, 3-17

Haley, J. (1973) *Uncommon therapy: The psychiatric techniques of Milton H. Erickson.* New York: Ballentine

Hall, M.P. (1954). *The essential nature of consciousness.* Los Angeles: Philosophical Research Society

Heisenberg, W. (1958). *Physics and philosophy.* New York: Harper & Row

Hillman, J. (1975). *Re-Visioning psychology.* New York: Harper & Row

Holt, P. (1997). "Hook Shots," in *San Francisco Chronicle*, May 6, 1997, p. E1-3

Huxley, A. (1944). *The perennial philosophy*. New York: Harper & Row

Idemon, R. (1996). *The Magic Thread.* York Beach, MN: Samuel Weiser, Inc.

Jung, C.G. (1959). *The Archetypes and the Collective Unconscious*. Collected Works, Vol. 9 (1), Bollin-gen Series XX. New York: Pantheon

Kant, I. (1968). *Critique of pure reason.* Translated by N.K. Smith. London: Macmillan

Klein, Jean. (1988). *Ease of being.* New York: Norton

Kovaleski, S. (1997). "Kaczynski's letters home paint a chilling portrait," in *San Francisco Chronicle, January 20, 1997, p. A4*

Krishnamurti, J. (1972). *You are the world.* New York: Harper & Row

May, R. (1969). *Love and will.* New York: Norton

McWaters, B. Conscious Evolution: Personal and planetary transformation. San Francisco, Ca: Evolutionary Press

Pearson, C. (1991). *Awakening the heroes within.* San Francisco, Ca.: Harper

Perry, G. (2012a). *Introduction to AstroPsychology.* Haddam Neck, CT: AAP Press

Perry, G. (2012b). *Depth Analysis of the Natal Chart.* Haddam Neck, CT: AAP Press

Rodman, D. (1996). *Bad as I wanna be.* New York: Dell

Rosenberg, M. (1979). *Conceiving the self.* New York: Basic Books

Rosenfeld, S. (1998). "Bomber: A tortured individual," in *San Francisco Examiner*, Sep. 13, 1998

Sasportas, H. (1989). *The gods of change.* London: Arkana, Penguin Books

Singer, J. (1972). *Boundaries of the soul.* Garden City, NY: Doubleday & Company

Smith, H. *Forgotten truth: The primordial tradition.* New York: Harper & Row

Stern, H. (1993). *Private parts.* New York: Pocket Books

Suzuki, D.T. (1968). *The essence of Buddhism.* Kyoto, Japan: Hozokan

Tarnas, R. (1995). *Prometheus the awakener.* Woodstock, Ct.: Spring Publications

Taylor, E. (1978). Asian Interpretations: Transcending the stream of consciousness. In K. Pope & J. Singer (Eds.), *The stream of consciousness.* New York: Plenum Press

Teilhard de Chardin, P. (1959). *The phenomenon of man.* New York: Harper & Row

Tompkins, S. (1989). *Aspects in astrology.* Rockport, Ma.: Element books Vogler, C. (1992). *The writers journey.* Studio City, Ca.: Michael Wiese Productions

Wagner, J. (1985). *The search for signs of intelligent life in the universe.* New York: Harper & Row

Watts, A. (1975). *Tao: The watercourse way.* New York: Pantheon

Welsford, E. (1961). *The Fool: This Social and Literary History.* Garden City, NY: Doubleday

Whitehead, A. (1920). *The concept of nature.* Cambridge: Cambridge University Press

Willeford, W. (1969). *The Fool and his scepter: A study in clowns and jesters and their audience.* Evanston, IL: Northwestern Univ. Press

Williamson, M. (1996). *A return to love: Reflections on the principles of a course in miracles.* New York: Harper Collins

Made in the USA
Charleston, SC
30 July 2013